Dear Payal and
Animon,

Many memories of
the land we came
from. Love,
Vrhiamma
Rajgffelu

# TRANSPLANTED

*From 110 Degrees in the Shade to*
*10 Degrees Below Zero in the Sun*

## Shakuntala Rajagopal

## Dedication

*To the kindest man I have ever known,*

*my daddy,*

*Photographer K.V. Sivaraam*

*Who would have been 'Appoo' to my girls*
*if they had the fortune to know him*

*I know he still keeps smiling upon me.*

*Shakuntala Rajagopal*

*Also by Shakuntala Rajagopal*

*Radha, a novel*

*Song of the Mountains,*

*My Pilgrimage to Maa Ganga*

*a Memoir*

# Table of Contents

# *An Invocation*

**I THANK LORD NARAYANA** for the yearning within me to tell my story of being transplanted in this soil, once foreign to me, and for nurturing my spirit to survive, nay, thrive and prosper, and make this country my own. I invoke the blessing of Lord Ganesha, the Divine Scribe, for the smooth flowing process of my storytelling, by removing any obstacles in my way. I invite Devi Saraswathi, the Goddess of learning, to play upon my tongue as I narrate my story, and humbly request her to enable me to transcribe my words upon these pages for all others to see.

# 1

## The Chenthitta House

***A Child is Welcomed to this World with Honey and Gold***

**NOVEMBER, 1945**

I was a five-year-old girl at the time.

I was startled awake from a deep sleep by the hustle and bustle of unusual activity, doors opening and closing, and many footsteps back and forth outside my ammoomma's, grandmother's, room where I slept alongside my three-year-old sister, Shanthi. Footsteps hurried across the floor. Listening closely, I heard more footsteps that paced back and forth outside my bedroom.

The clock said 2:00 a.m. I was glad that somebody remembered to leave the blue night light on.

Suddenly a new sound pierced the night. A wailing sound of a baby crying. I got up and off the bed and walked out of the room and straight into the arms of my maternal aunt, Ammachi. She explained what I heard was a baby's first announcement of its arrival, a demanding cry—a craving for attention. The craving was quite evident (a craving I have come to believe ends only with our last breath). I ran toward the room where the sound came from. I could not wait any longer to be called. (In our household an obedient child never interrupted adults unless expressly summoned!) Thank God everyone was too busy; too happy to be strict at that point. I barely heard my ammachi's voice, something about a new sister. And then I saw her—a squiggly baby, shining-wet after her first bath, still screaming, and oh so small.

So, this was my new baby sister. I pushed forward to see her face. I was sure she looked straight at me. My five-year-old heart swelled with love for her instantly.

The adults were still bustling around preparing an official welcome for the new addition to the family. As was our custom in South India, my ammoomma, the oldest member of the family present, was going to feed the little one three sips of honey and gold. I saw Ammachi rub a piece of gold, my mother's wedding ring, into a few drops of honey placed in a little white marble boat. I recognized it as the marble mortar in which our medicine pills were ground up to feed us medicines. The sweetest food of all, honey, and the most precious metal of all, gold--a mixture that is a symbolic offering of the best in life to the new and smallest member of our family, by the senior-most family member, Ammoomma.

But not this time. I was vehement; she was 'my' sister. I wanted to officially welcome her, and, boy, I wasn't going to settle for a nay answer. I must have won my point because this time they waived tradition. Soon I had the squirming little sister in my lap. My small hands needed help to keep her there. I held the bundle of joy while grandma had to lean down to feed her the gold and honey. Everybody smiled. Dad shook his head in disbelief. My ammoomma was not one to give in to anyone. But she did for me, her special *kochu-mol,* granddaughter.

The sweet stuff must have made an impression on the little one, for she soon settled quietly in her big sister's arms as I sighed in relief and sat back; basking in the sunshine of all the attention I was sharing with my own baby sister.

That was the very special place where my two sisters and I grew up with my parents, and my ammachi, my maternal aunt, when I was a child.

Sixty-eight years later, I really believe that the sense of belonging, the sense of unconditional love and the sense of ultimate trust in placing a live human being in my hands--all these added up to what I became when I grew up from my five-year-old self.

### *Re-visiting The Chenthitta House, 06-11-2013*

My beloved childhood home stood empty and abandoned in the middle of the sleepy seaside town of Thiruananthapuram in South India, in the area of town named *Chenthitta.*

Fifty years ago I had left that house for the United States. *The Chenthitta house* is where my ammoomma--grandmother, raised her family. Since then, the family was forced to move because the railroad authorities had acquired the house when the national railroad was extended to go further south to the tip of India, fifty miles away. The new railway tracks passed too close to the house and raised safety issues.

In 2013, on a hot afternoon in June, for the first time I took my young grandson, Travis, to see the house I grew up in. We were accompanied by his mother, Devi, my eldest daughter, and his father, Don.

"At least it is still standing, so even today we get to see it," Travis piped up.

We drove up to *The Chenthitta house*, but could not go in. Piles of bricks, broken twigs, dry leaves and flying paper filled most of the front yard, blocking the door to what was our drawing room, as the living room was called.

Being on a busy street that led onto a highway, I remembered we had always kept the front gates closed. Two large heavy metal gates separated the house from the street and were large enough to let in a car. They touted a fancy scrolled design on the top, and they swung inward to open. It used to be that the only time those gates were opened would be to let a car in or out. In the middle of the larger gates was a central doorway with smaller, regular-sized doors that opened into the front yard. Even these walk-in doors used to be kept locked when we lived there. But now I saw these smaller doors were wide open and hanging loosely on their hinges. Even the right larger gate was partly open. The house was obviously unoccupied and sadly abandoned. We pushed open one gate. The gate swung wide open, but we could not enter the front yard. Broken bricks, tree branches, and all sorts of debris blocked our path. Our small group of family members was quite disappointed.

I saw it was not safe to push any further. But I had a solution.

I knew that on the elevated lot to the right side of the house where I grew up, there existed a temple for Lord Shiva. If the temple was open we would be able to look at the house from a good vantage point. When I was young, the temple belonged to a private family, and they held Pooja services only on weekends.

The Temple had been in disrepair as long as I can remember. The temple yard had a small clearing around the sanctum where the idol was housed. But the rest of the yard was overcome by weeds, filled with wild grass and unkempt rose bushes.

My ammoomma sponsored Pooja services there once a week, to honor the deity of Lord Shiva. On those occasions we went in from the street entrance to pray to Lord Shiva.

I had a history with the temple. Being that the temple lot was at an elevation from the road level, I recalled how we propped up a ladder against our garage wall, which allowed me, along with my sister, Shanti, and our cousin, Babu Chettan, to climb onto the terraced roof of the garage. We also coerced our all-around helper/runner boy Madhavan to do so with us. Then we would jump down a few feet to the temple yard and collect hibiscus, oleander, and some other wild flowers that grew there. With these we decorated the deities in our Pooja room. We did this a couple of times each summer vacation. At the time of our annual Onam festival, we needed lots of flowers for the floral designs we made in our front yard. We felt free to climb over and pick more flowers. There were blooming bushes of **poochedi poovu, or** Lantana which bloomed almost all summer with orange and yellow blossoms. Around August- September, dark purplish blue berries appeared, each berry less than a quarter inch in size and clustered in bunches of a dozen or so. In a day or two the birds ate the bushes clean. These berries are edible, sweet and juicy, and when we were lucky, we got to pick them before the birds polished them off.

Getting back onto the wall from the other side was a little tricky. We stepped on a rock or tree stump and helped each other. An occasional scraped knee or arm was our secret until bath-time. We were warned to avoid poison ivy, but not forbidden to climb over again.

My grander memory of this temple yard was the **bubblimass** *tree,* the pink-grapefruit tree, with unique wide glossy leaves. The tree bore fruit just twice a year. The pink grapefruits could be seen at eye level from my bedroom, making it very tempting to go pick them. Although the bitter-sweet-sour taste was not my favorite, the challenge of getting the fruit intrigued me. It was not that I could not climb the tree. I knew I could do it. But if any of my ammoomma's patients saw me up on that tree, and she heard about it through them, I would be shaming her. So I did not climb the *bubblimass* tree. When in season, it was Babu Chettan or Madhavan who helped us pick the fruit. Once we climbed over the wall, they would pull up the ladder and use it to reach the taller branches of the *bubblimass tree* where the best fruit were.

The challenge was not in getting the fruit, but to accomplish all this within a slot of time when my ammoomma, grandmother, or my ammachi, maternal aunt, were not home.

My ammoomma went to the hospital at 8.00 a.m. and Ammachi to her chemistry department at the university at 9.00 a.m. Ammoomma could return for lunch anytime between 11.30 a.m. to 12.30 p.m. In between, we had to catch Madhavan to help between his chores of going to the Chalai Market to buy fresh fish, to the butcher's to pick up the order already placed for goat-meat, or to the provision-store for oil, flour etc.

We somehow managed to squeeze in enough time to pick the fruit. Nobody else came to pick it, so we did not feel guilty. The perfect round balls of what looked like a cross between an orange and super-size lemon reflected tints of pink on its skin. Each was about four inches in diameter, and we took turns carrying them over the temple wall, and down the properly placed ladder. We could not wait to see the glistening pink flesh of the ripe fruit when cut in half. I remember the ant-bites from the large red ants on the *bubblimass* tree--none of could escape that, but I don't remember any of us falling off the ladder in any of our escapades.

I was aware that since that time the temple and yard had been donated to the governmental temple authorities. The walls and yard had been cleaned up, and regular *Pooja* services were offered there.

As I was telling Travis about the possibility of viewing the Chenthitta house from the temple yard, we heard the temple bells peeling in the air. The sounds welcomed us.

We walked around the corner to the temple, climbed up about a dozen steps to say a prayer to Lord Shiva, and after doing our prostrations in front of the deity; we got to the business of trying to check out my old house from the temple grounds.

In my native language, Malayalam, there is a saying, *"Naadu marannalum, veedu marakkaruthu."* It means, "Even if you forget your land, don't forget your home, your roots."

I can in no way forget my land, India, and never could I forget my home, where my roots are.

When I say 'roots,' I mean my **Chenthitta house,** the house where I grew up. It was my ammoomma*'s* house, where I lived until I got married at age twenty-three and moved to my husband's home, which then became my home.

I had to grow up twice. The first time, growing up was a pleasure in the bosom of a warm extended family. By any standard, I was spoiled rotten. There were so many people and so much love, it could not be avoided; they all spoiled me, the first-born of my generation in my ammoomma's home.

Later, as a young woman in my early twenties I had to grow up in this land for a second time. Although I was twenty-three years old when I joined my husband in the USA, I had to learn life all over again to survive the strange climate changes, the totally different food and the different vocabulary and way of life in this strange land.

Travis had heard many tales of my **Doctor Ammoomma** during his sleep-overs. My ammoomma was a matriarch with two faces.

In 1946, I was six years old and a central character within a large extended family, of which the matriarchal head was Dr. J.V. Chellamma, my ammoomma, who also happened to be a practicing physician.

To the world at large she was the tough grandmother who disciplined her children, grandchildren, nieces, nephews, and the household help with an iron hand and a stern voice to match.

To me, her special and oldest granddaughter, she was an angel of mercy and an agent of love. I received my share of spankings and discipline at times, but the love and caring she showed to my parents, and the fun trips reserved just for us, made up for all of it.

My sister, Shanthi, and I slept in my ammoomma's bedroom on mattresses which were rolled up and put away during the day. One morning I woke up to find my ammoomma's bed empty. I was told she had been called to the hospital for a delivery late at night. It intrigued and excited me that her job involved taking care of pregnant ladies and that she delivered their babies. I enjoyed watching the babies when the mothers came for their check-ups after the babies were born.

That morning I sat on the front steps of our house and waited for her to come back. The sun had come up, and it was already getting hot as I waited for her return. After some time, the gates opened and she walked in, the peon from the hospital carrying an umbrella over her against the sun. She was an important doctor on the staff, and never went anywhere alone and never needed to carry her own umbrella or even her own black doctor-bag.

She looked tired; it must have been a long night. I jumped up and ran into her welcoming arms. I was happy to see her, but I think she was even more pleased to see me. Her curly hair was tied back into a bun as usual. But, unlike the fully controlled 'no hair out of place' look that she usually maintained, she was a little disheveled, her crisp white saree had crumpled in places. I'd never seen her in such disarray and it upset me. I grabbed on to her and asked if something bad had happened. She took my hand, walked into the drawing room, and sat on the big couch, gathering me close to her. "Nothing bad happened, Paapa (my nickname). I had to deliver twin babies last night."

"Are they okay?" I was curious.

Maybe because I had already made up my mind to become a doctor (I'd called myself *Dr. Paapa* since I was three), or maybe she was in a generous mood, she explained to me how the mother was bleeding badly (much more than when I had cut myself with the kitchen knife last month), and how she and the assisting midwife had to hurry and help the babies to come out one by one, without hurting the mother. "And," she added with a sigh of relief, "I sewed her up to stop her bleeding."

"With a needle and thread?"

"Yes." She was laughing now. Not a loud laugh, but a dignified chuckle. "It was okay. I took good care of her. She and the babies are fine."

She rose to her feet, lifting me up with her. "Run along and get ready for school. I need to take a bath, eat breakfast, and go back to the hospital to make rounds on my other patients."

Kamalakshy chechi, the cook, made her coffee and took it to her room the minute she returned from the hospital. Her assistant was already warming water for her bath. Ammachi, my maternal aunt, had already lain out on her four poster bed a white cotton blouse and saree for her to change into. The finely woven cotton towel she used after her bath hung on the clothesline just outside her room.

Ammoomma undid her hairpins and released her long, dark, wavy hair which fell down to her waist. I wished she would not tie it back up. But I suppose she had to look dignified for her patients and their families. I later found out it was the rule in the hospital that all long hair be tied up so it did not touch patients' beds.

Kamalakshy chechi handed Ammoomma a small steel bowl of warm oil. The special coconut oil in which black peppercorns had been fried previously was sieved and cleared before use. Treating the oil in such a way rendered the scalp healthy and kept the long hair thick and shiny, I had been told. Ammoomma rubbed the oil on to her scalp and hair and grabbed her towel on her way to take her bath.

When she returned, all freshened and changed into her crisp white saree, I was already eating my breakfast of idlis, steamed rice cakes, and sambar, a mixed vegetable curry with spicy red peppers and strong curry leaves that smelled up the whole house with aromas that made even the pickiest eater hungry. A large round steel plate was placed in front of her and idlis and sambar were served with reverence and care. Reverence because Ammoomma was the matriarch and breadwinner, and extra care because any spill would be ensued by a good whack on the head of the server. My ammoomma had a really bad temper.

She sat at the table like a queen on a throne, her hair hanging loose over her shoulders. She let it dry while she ate, making her look kind and easygoing, the way I liked her. Later, when it was tied back into a bun, her face would transform to the severe taskmaster and disciplinarian who ruled home and hospital alike. Even her eating changed with this attire: straight back, intent eyes, and deft motion of fingers as she quickly fingered pieces of soft idlis, dipped them into the sambar sauce, and gracefully scooped them into her mouth. Now a cup of steaming hot coffee appeared in front of her and one teaspoon of sugar was added under her supervision. She nodded to Kamalakshy chechi to give me coffee also. I was given a *'paal-kaapi,' milk-coffee*, more milk than coffee, with one spoon of sugar added. No less, no more.

When both of us were done with breakfast she went to her room to draw her hair back, powder her face, place the 'pottu,' dot that Hindus wear on her forehead, and get her doctor bag together. I helped her place her stethoscope in the bag. But before I did, I put the earpieces to my ears and placed the disc on my chest to listen to my heart, which she had taught me to do. From the corner of my eyes, I saw her smiling, something she didn't do often. She never laughed out loud. I suppose she needed to keep up appearances.

We left the house together with the hospital peon who had come to escort her. At the corner by our house I boarded the school bus, while she walked on to the Women and Children's Hospital across from the bus stop. When I turned around, I saw my ammoomma looking at me with a soft sweet smile and kind loving eyes. To me she was not the stern Dr. Chellamma that she was to the rest of the world.

The Chenthitta house.

Shakuntala, Jayee and Shanthi, 1945

# 2

# The Chenthitta House (continued......)

**MY DAUGHTER DEVI'S** younger son, Travis, loved being half Indian and took pride in listening to stories of my ammoomma and me. He also took the time to look up his father's Italian ancestry, *Romano,* as well as the English lineage, *Kingston*. Just after Travis turned two, my husband Raj and I moved five houses away from my daughter Devi's house, so Travis grew up close to both of us. We were already very close to my only other grandchild, Niko, Devi's oldest son because they had lived with us for over four years from Niko's three years of age to seven years. Raj and I were blessed that both our grandchildren were always in our lives.

Travis was getting anxious to hear about the Chenthitta house and hear all about the time I lived there. But the ritual of paying our respects to the deity had to come first.

Once we had entered the temple grounds we proceeded to pray to the deity, Lord Shiva the destroyer God. For without destroying the old and unsavory, there would be no chance for more good and new to arise.

After we had said our prayers at the sanctum of Shiva, we walked over to the wall that separated my ammoomma's old house and the

Shiva temple. It was good to see the temple grounds clean and sandy, with stone paths separating flower beds, jasmine in bloom, oleanders of three different colors, deep pink, light pink, and creamy white blooms, and red and yellow hibiscus, all reflecting the glorious summer season, already blessed by the rains from the beginning of the monsoon season.

By contrast, the Chenthitta house, no longer mine or my grandmother's, was in appalling disrepair. I tried to hide my shock and my tears from Travis as well as I could.

Straight ahead from where we stood by the north end of the wall, I showed Travis the front veranda with four crescent-moon-shaped cement steps, quite well preserved despite years of neglect. The door to the drawing room was closed. Through two open windows we could peek into that room. We could see part of the floor inside, and piles of paper on the floor as well as on what appeared to be table tops. I described to him that the floor used to be dark grey polished cement. Such a floor was cool to the feet in the hot sub-tropical weather. I told him how my ammoomma's house was one of the first ones in town that had colors painted outside when weather resistant paints were first available in the early fifties. Ammoomma chose a mauve-pink and moss-green façade. Past the front steps, facing the main street, there was a curved wall, about ten feet wide and two stories tall that had a fluted appearance. Here too the color on the wall was a mauve-pink hue. This type of colorful exterior was totally new for residences in the area when Ammoomma had the house built in 1950, when the main house which had been one story tall and quite old, had been torn down and rebuilt. My heart ached to see that the colors had been painted over with an off-white color. But this layer had peeled off and in many places the original colors showed, but faded and patchy.

The people in charge and the passing of time were both cruel to the once beautiful and well maintained wall.

Sixty-three years later my grandson was asking me to show him the bedroom in which my sister and I slept in. We could see into the second floor window and although not well lit, the room appeared to be empty.

Just outside my old room was a round balcony facing the front yard and the road. I pointed out the huge mango tree that had branches over the balcony in front of the bedroom Shanthi and I once shared. I told Travis that as a girl I had wished and waited for that tree to give fruit. It was amazing that it was still alive. The old mango tree in the front yard had not borne any fruit in many years, but it still cast shade over the front portico and the circular terrace over the portico roof.

He asked his father to video tape my description of the house, its new and old sections, and my stories of life at the Chenthitta house.

Walking around the temple ground, I was able to find a right spot by the temple yard to point out to Travis the narrow concrete steps to the terraced roof above the second floor. That is where I went to read my books undisturbed. There was only one problem with that. I could not hear anyone when I was called to come down to say our evening prayers and then to have supper. It was the only time I ever got in trouble. It was too difficult for the older members of my family to climb upstairs to pluck me out of the world of books I was immersed in. When I told him the story, Travis had a good chuckle picturing my being scolded by my ammoomma.

From the South end of the temple grounds, where we stood closest to the roof of the garage in my Chenthitta house, I pointed out to Travis that the original part of the house was not torn down when the new house was built, and he immediately remembered that I'd previously told him stories of how that part was over one hundred years old. Travis loved everything old. He was always fascinated to hear how I grew up in a different land. Now he was seeing and experiencing the world of my youth. Now I was *his* Doctor Ammoomma.

Travis already knew how it was in this older section of the house, that one room was a designated birthing room. Often in the *birthing suite* we had a constant flow of mini-families in residence too. More than two times a year, close relatives like my mother's cousin, stayed there when she was ready to have her baby. Once she delivered the baby, she'd stay on for ten or twelve days before she returned home. The mother and child, and her own mother or maternity-helper that came with her, would all be fed and watched over by our own household help. The ladies in the kitchen were always busy. If it was a complicated case, the expectant mother was transferred to the Thycaud Women and Childrens' Hospital, a block away.

For the delivery at home, my ammoomma had a midwife help her. Subhadramma was part of the family and a favorite aunty to me when I was young.

I pointed out the door at the end of the front veranda which opened to my ammoomma's exam room where she saw her patients. I explained how that room had its own separate entrance so that the patients did not come through the main house. But after a few years of knowing a patient and his or her family, friendships formed, some casual, many close, so that the rest of us came to know them quite well also.

Although quite an independent soul, even my ammoomma did not travel around town alone. Either a brother or a close friend went with her on her house visits, whether the patient's home was within walking distance or not. Firstly, decorum and personal safety called for her to be escorted, being that she was a VIP in her own right. The patient's family usually brought the transportation for the house calls if she had to travel more than a block or so from our house. Only a few of them had their own cars; most often they came in a taxi-car to fetch her. On those occasions when she was going to a home where the children or grandchildren were of my age, she allowed me to go with her, and I visited while she did her doctoring. I have been told that at the age of three I started carrying her stethoscope around and called myself *Doctor Pāāpa,* my pet name.

My ammoomma was the second of eight siblings. Born to a land-owner farmer, it was her uncle who saw her potential and enrolled her in Vellore Christian Medical College in 1913 for her medical training. She was determined to go to medicine and convinced her uncle she could do it by her good grades in school as well as her persistence in attending school against all odds. When she became a teenager, she was expected to quit school and stay home to help take care of her younger siblings.

The Chenthitta house bustled with people. It was true communal living with four generations under the same roof.

When her father died, she brought her stepmother to live with her. The stepmother was a petite woman who Ammoomma's father married for the sole purpose of managing his three young children under ten years of age after his first wife died.

Ammoomma's youngest brother, my mother's uncle, six years old at the time, was included in the move, and lived with us.

Then there was my mother, my father, my sister Shanthi and me.

My mother's older sister, I called her *Ammachi,* and their younger brother, *my* uncle, who was a dentist, also lived the Chenthitta house. The way each of them took care of each other was an amazing experience to observe. Ammoomma, Ammachi, and my father had to leave early to go to their jobs. My uncle went to his dental office a little later. My great uncle, Ammoomma's brother, was not a good student and did not go to school. He went to the rice-fields we owned to supervise the paddy workers and usually came back at sundown, after he paid their wages.

There was, of course, a cook who lived with us. The lady who cleaned house and washed clothes was a day worker. There was also Go-fer, a young boy who was the cook's helper who went to the market every day and did all sorts of errands for everyone in the house.

I loved the fact that my mother stayed home. She made sure everyone got fed on time, got their clothes ironed and ready, and once all of us left for work or school, she packed lunches for the adults. Tiffin carriers which were two or three tiered aluminum containers with rods on both sides keeping them tightly packed together contained rice, vegetable curry, another vegetable dish, and sometimes chicken or mutton curry in each carrier. The lunches were then transported to the different offices at the other end of town by the young man on a bicycle with a carrier rack in the back. Each member cared for the others' needs by working and providing for each other with wholehearted devotion, grace and kindness.

My ammoomma worked at the hospital, and since it was only a

block away she usually came home for lunch between morning rounds where she saw inpatients and the afternoon clinic where she took care of outpatients.

If she got very busy delivering babies, she would send the hospital *peon* to get her lunch from the house. Along with the hefty dose of love, affection, and joy came the bonds of responsibility and account-ability, and above all an inherent need *to give.*

The adults in my life, it just so happened, uniformly reveled in *giving.*

The year that I turned eight, my ammoomma had a house built for my mom and dad, only a mile away from the Chenthitta House, with a yard complete with mango trees and coconut palms. There were huge shade trees of jackfruit and tamarind, which we could climb on, and from which wooden swings on long ropes absolutely enthralled us. With four bedrooms, a separate prayer room, and a large kitchen, it was close to perfect. What really made it perfect was how close it was to ammoomma's home, and within walking distance for easy visiting. Even though the house was that close by, my dad felt that it was not fair to take away ammoomma's two bundles of joy from his mother-in-law. So, my Mom and Dad moved into the new house with my youngest sister, Jayee, who was three, while my sister Shanthi, who was six, and myself stayed and lived with Ammoomma, with Ammachi in charge of us.

It was not traumatic for us because we had the best of the whole arrangement. Mom's house was only a mile away, and every evening after dinner, Dad and Mom walked over to ammoomma's, and spent time with us. Mom helped to get us ready for bed, and then returned to her home.

I did not realize until I had my daughters how big of a sacrifice my mom made in allowing us to stay with Ammoomma. But Dad felt it was not right to separate us from Ammoomma because she was very attached to us. And, Mom agreed. I would not even send my daugh-ters away to camp when they were young; I still missed my sisters so much, I did not want to be separated from my young ones for even the few days of a summer camp.

Travis understood how strongly I felt about all the people I had left behind when I settled here in the USA. He hugged me tight as we left the temple grounds. His hug made up for many other hugs I had missed from all those loved ones

Ammoomma and me with her stethoscope.1943

June 2013 Devi, Travis and Shaku. Chenthitta house in background, viewed from the Shiva temple-grounds. The steps to "My terrace" are seen on the upper right corner.

*3*

# Where Two Bee Hives Stood Sentinel, While We Sisters Played.

**HONEYBEES ARE SPECIAL** to me because I love ho ney on toast, on *puttu* a regular breakfast food  made of steamed rice flour and grated coconut, and even on sliced bananas. So, recently when I read about how the bees are at risk, I worried about what will happen to my honey supply. But more significantly, if honeybees disappear, the yield of different fruits, vegetables and other food crops will decrease by 30 to 40 percent universally. That would pose a serious problem for the entire world.

I do my part, albeit in a small way, to help honey bees. My patch of Monarda or Bee Balm, my patches of lavender, and even my apple trees provide haven to many kinds of bees, including honeybees.

Honeybee feasting on my Lavenders.

A few years ago, a bee flew into my can of diet coke, and stung my lower lip, which ended up looking like I had enhancement surgery. But it did not last long.

All this takes me back to many moons ago when Shanti and I lived at the Chenthitta House, and we played around some bee hives.

The center of my existence at that time was a courtyard where two beehives stood at attention between a fig tree and a breezeway that led from a kitchen work area to a bathroom. This bathroom had a window that opened to a drawing well, complete with a pulley, rope, and draw bucket.

I was five years old, I remember, because it was the year my mother presented me with one more sister, and it was also the year that I started kindergarten.

On the far end, this gardened area was bounded by a brick wall, maybe five feet tall, which separated the hustle and bustle of a road that went from the center of Thiruananthapuram town to the Chalai market, and onto the main highway which took you all the way to the southern tip of India, Kanya Kumari, also known as Cape Coumarin.

The opposite end of this garden was defined by the above-mentioned breezeway. Parapet walls on both sides of the breezeway provided welcome seating. Shanthi and I would sit on these low walls and watch my amma and Ammachi tend their garden. We saw flowers touting a variety of colors from the sparkling white jasmines to the pale lavender cosmos, and bright yellow chrysanthemums. The smooth petals of the pink roses contrasted with the prickly thorns, which effectively kept them safe from two busy little girls who could not keep their hands off of any blooming thing. The pleasant bouquet of jasmines and roses blended with the strong scents of chrysanthemums. The pink oleanders were not planted in this area because their pungent odor was not welcome here. They were in the front yard where their huge bushes rubbed shoulders with the mighty hibiscus plants.

To the left of us were two long steps leading to a door of Doctor Ammoomma's bedroom. Her four poster bed was made of dark mahogany. I loved to run my fingers over the smooth shiny curves of the bedframe, and follow the grooves of the scrolls in the design of the headboard. A dresser and table of the same wood sat beside her bed, and her stethoscope rested atop the table when she was home. This was also the room where Shanthi and I slept on the floor, on mattresses that unfolded at bedtime and were then rolled and put away during the day.

Also on the floor, our *Adukkala ammoomma*, kitchen grandmother, slept beside us. Although I was aware that she oversaw the kitchen ladies at their tasks (hence the name kitchen grandmother), and the errand boy who went to the market for fish every day, I felt that she was my own guardian angel who looked after me. Adukkala ammoomma made sure I ate the last ball of rice and curds on my plate. She was the one who urged me to finish my daily alphabet-writing-practice before I got into trouble with my ammachi when she returned from the university.

The bathroom wall formed the fourth boundary for this delightful corner of my world at five. Entering the bathroom from the breezeway, you saw a window in the wall to the right. This window opened to a well we used to draw water into a huge clay pot set atop a wood-burning stove to heat the water for bathing. When the window was closed for privacy, the rope and bucket attached to the well were swung to the outer half of the water-well. Here the amenities included separate areas for washing clothes, and for washing kitchen pots and utensils. There was a spot here as well for cleaning the fresh fish from the market, sometimes twice in one day.

1941.  My mother drawing water from the well
through the bathroom window.

I was fascinated by the way the wood-burning stove for heating the bathwater worked. It was set half inside and half outside the bathroom wall, and the wood was fed from outside the bathroom. The inside half had the rim built to hold the large pot of water. A chimney set up above this stove took the smoke out of the bathroom itself. Looking back, the ingenuity and the engineering were marvels that I was too young to appreciate.

Every three months or so, the *theineechakaran*, honey-bee-man, came. He wore a pant-suit and boots covering his entire body. He placed a large brimmed hat on his head, and pulled down the protective netting around his face and neck. Long gloves completed his work habit. We were allowed to watch from Doctor Ammoomma's bedroom window while he expertly smoked the bees into a box he carried. Once the queen bee was in his trap, he waved to us. We were then allowed to go out and see how he gingerly picked up honey combs, placed them in his barrel with a handle on the outside that he cranked (a manual centrifuge of sorts), and extracted the honey into dripping pans through cotton-lined sieves. When one hive was done, he would give us pieces of the honeycomb to suck out drops of honey from the crannies. Then he chased us back inside and proceeded to retrieve the honey from the second one. Once we had some honey to savor, we lost interest in the proceedings. But, to finish our lesson, Ammachi called us back to see the honey-man place the queen bee back into the bee hive, and showed us how the remaining bees swarmed back in without further ado. Ammachi did not waste any occasion to feed our brain, even as our tummies were fed.

I was fascinated by how the queen bee ruled the worker bees and drones to maintain order in the colony.

The fig tree only gave fruit occasionally, probably once or twice a year. But each time it did, the anticipation on Ammachi's face as she awaited their ripening was a family joke. When the fruit was of a certain size, she'd wrap them with gauze to protect them from the crows. Each ripe fruit was tenderly sliced, and she ruefully shared them with us. I still remember my amma declining her share, so that Ammachi, her sister, could have more. They were close then.

My gardens in this part of the continent, with its harsh winters, could not sustain the tropical blooms or a fig tree. They thrive in my heart and mind, always.

At times, in the deep freeze of January, when grey skies cloud over me and all of Chicago-land is blanketed by miles and miles of white snow, when even the green tops of tall evergreens have turned snow-white, the chill seeps into my heart and drags me down. I close my eyes and see the patch of sunlight upon the beehives, and hear my ammachi calling, "Pāāpa --, thein veno?" (Pāāpa, that's me, do you want some honey?), and my whole being warms up with the love from that sunny corner of the earth decades ago.

Shaku in Dad's Greeting card, January 1945

# 4

## Kindergarten

THE EARLIEST MENTAL picture of my father was the day he enrolled me in the kindergarten class at Holy Angels Convent School. I wore a floral dress, white socks, and black shoes. In later years there would be a school uniform at this school, but this wasn't the case when I was enrolled. Daddy was humming a tune as we stepped out of the taxi car in front of my new school. There was always a prayer on his lips, usually a tune from one of the Krishna prayers we children chanted at dusk every day.

We walked across a huge sandy playground where some older girls mulled around the edge of the large shade trees, and where some small boys around my age were being led toward a large building at the end of the playground. A few feet before the front doors to that large building, I saw a rock formation almost like the face of a cave, and a few steps deep at the center. There I recognized the statue of Mother Mary, Her right hand raised in a blessing and the left hand holding a string of rosary beads. I recognized the area as a grotto. I had seen such a grotto by the chapel in the nunnery adjacent to Ammoomma's hospital. Many of the nuns in that hospital were nurses who worked with my ammoomma. I said to my father, "Wait, wait," and ran over and knelt in prayer by Mother Mary for a few minutes, then ran back to my father. The nuns at the hospital had taught me well. My father laughed as he took my hand and led me to a room to the left of the larger building and behind the grotto.

At that age I followed what my dad and my ammoomma had taught me--to respect Divinity in any name or form. As I grew older I learned how liberal my Hindu religion was. It did not prevent me from honoring other religions and taught me to respect other religious choices. It took me years to realize how progressive a thinker my father was. He had taken me to this particular school run by the French order of nuns, where only very few of the nuns spoke my native language, Malayalam. He was doing this to give me a good solid education and armed me with the universal language of English. In 1945, we were at the peak of the fight for freedom from the British rule, and my amma-chi told me how my dad wanted me to learn to think in English so I can be strong to fight against the British. If I had the opportunity to study Catholicism, he considered that an added bonus.

We were seated comfortably by the desk, across from the principal's chair and I noticed the principal was a nun. The black habit and the white collar muted me, and I was not my talkative self. I was used to the nuns working at the hospital under my Ammoomma; they wore the nurses' uniforms most of the time. The nuns knew me there as a special visitor because I was Ammoomma's grandchild. In the principal's office I felt the importance of authority to which I must afford respect, yet something felt strange. It was a different feeling from my parents' or Ammoomma's rules. I could not figure it out; perhaps it was the principal's authoritative presence and her black habit.

After my father signed a few papers, the principal stood up and walked over to my chair. "So, you are Shakuntala?"

I nodded yes.

"You will be in Sr. Adelaide's kindergarten class. Hope you learn a lot."

She shook hands with me and let me down from the chair. I said, "Thank you." She smiled.

Dad took my hand and we followed a girl bigger than me who wore a long plain dress in gray cotton. She wore no jewelry. Feeling a little self-conscious, I touched my butterfly pendant which I wore at all times. My mother told me the body and the head of the butterfly pendant were opals, my birthstone. As time passed I found out that this girl was one of a dozen orphans whom the nuns raised and educated in the convent.

We backtracked our way past the grotto, the playground, and a small garden of flowers. I stopped to look at the roses in the garden and saw a beautiful building with an angled roof and  large ornate doors. The girl who was guiding us told me it was the convent chapel.

As we neared the parking lot where a few cars and the school bus were parked, the girl pointed toward a small cottage-like building. It was set back from the traffic area. My fingers tightened around my father's as we walked down a few steps to it. It looked quite welcoming with flower-beds touting red hibiscus and yellow chrysanthemums. The right corner of the building shelved a full lush vine that had climbed up a post and onto the low roof's edge. With pride I whispered to my father it was a jasmine. We caught the sweet smell of yesterday's flowers. I knew they bloomed at dusk and then shed, lasting only one day. Through the open windows I heard the chatter of other children and I perked up. In the doorway of the classroom a tall nun stood wearing a black habit like the principal wore, but unlike the principal --she stood smiling. My eyes focused on the long rosary chain she wore around her neck. She lifted the end of the chain and showed me a locket of a cross with the figure of a man on the cross. "Hello Shakuntala, I am Sr. Adelaide. Do you recognize the cross?"

"Yes, I answered." I was only too pleased to let her know it was Jesus Christ on the cross. I was not tongue-tied anymore.

The school bell started clanging in the distance and Sr. Adelaide said goodbye to my father and led me into the classroom. Before she could take me in, I ran back to hug my father. "Tata. Daddy!" I said, not too sure I wanted to be left there. He hugged me and reassured me he would be back for me at 3:00 p.m. I nodded. I went inside and ran to a window to wave goodbye to him. I did not want him to go, even though I knew he would keep his promise and come back.

Then I turned around to face a dozen or so classmates, mostly girls and three or four boys who said in unison, "Welcome to kindergarten, Shakuntala."

The *Grotto* in Holy Angels Convent High School.

# 5

## Dr. Chellamma's Family Saga

AROUND THE TIME my mom moved to her new house, I realized she called my ammoomma *'Valiamma.'* Valiamma means mother's older sister. I couldn't understand this. Wasn't my 'doctor *ammoomma'* her *'Amma,'* meaning mother? When I questioned her, she laughed.

"You mean all these years nobody told you our story?" For eight years of my life I had not known or questioned this. Mom sat down on the moon-shaped steps by the front veranda and pointed for me to sit by her before she started talking.

"When your ammoomma, (Dr. Chellamma) came back from Vellore Christian Medical College and started working at a local hospital near Kaudiar, a few miles away from town, her father arranged for her to be married to a lawyer, who was a relative. After her marriage she moved to her husband's house."

While she was away studying medicine, her older sister, Gauri Amma, and her younger sister Ponnamma, were married and started their families in their respective husband's home as is customary.

Dr. J. V. Chellamma, was my real ammoomma, but not my birth ammoomma. She was the second daughter of a landowner/farmer of Mazhavancheril House in Kaudiar, Trivandrum. Her parents, Janaki and Velayudhan, had a total of eight children, four daughters and four sons. Her mother died unexpectedly during the childbirth of a premature baby who also did not survive. Her father was devastated by the loss of his wife and child, and was overwhelmed in his new position of managing a household, his young children, his farms, and other businesses.

A year after Chellamma's mother died, her father married a much younger woman, basically to help raise the four boys, who were still ten and under at the time. Although a very sweet and kind lady  good in caring for the children, she was not able to manage the household or take care of her husband's landowner responsibilities. During this time, Chellamma learned her husband had a mental illness, probably schizophrenia, and needed to be admitted to a mental asylum. A few months into her father's marriage he fell ill, and Dr. Chellamma felt obligated to move back into the family home to manage her father's affairs. Her father was relieved and glad to relinquish the reins of all his interests to Chellamma. Smart and strong-willed, she found the right people to manage the farmers who worked in her father's farms and other land leased for cultivation. She kept the family together and all their riches.

In a way she was happy to return home, since she lived alone while her mentally ill spouse was living as an inpatient at the mental asylum.

I was curious. "Mom, wasn't she sad to leave her husband?"

"Yes, of course, mol. Yet, she felt she was needed more in her father's home at the time."

Three years went by and Chellamma's father fell ill again, and after a short illness he passed away. Now the stepmother also became her responsibility. Three brothers were in their teens, and the fourth was only seven years old. She not only had to manage the kids and the household, but in addition, her married sisters looked up to her as a mother figure when they needed guidance.

"Tragedy struck again," my mother continued. "Ponnamma [the younger sister] already had two children by the time Chellamma returned from Vellore Medical College. Her children were Saradamma and me." This was the first time I'd heard that Doctor Ammoomma's younger sister was really my birth grandmother.

"But Mom, we live with Doctor Ammoomma and she treats us as her own children and grandchildren." I was surprised not by the fact that I did not know this, but also by the way we were truly our Ammoomma's family and why she treated us as her own. It also became clear as to why the rest of the world, including relatives, as well as friends, referred to us as her children and grandchildren.

"That is because Doctor Ammoomma raised us as her own," Mom continued. "This time, sad things happened to my own mother, Ponnamma. She had married young and by now had three children, including me. My mother's father, my birth-grandfather, had gone to Mesopotamia as a mercenary. My mother did not know what war was going on there at the time. All she knew was that when her father returned home he was suffering with tuberculosis. Doctor Chellamma, as able and magnanimous as she was, invited them all back into her huge house smack in the middle of Kaudiar town.

"Ammoomma was indeed a smart woman. When her brother-in-law came home from Mesopotamia with a bag of money, instead of letting him spend it all on the family right away, she helped him buy some land. I think my mother told me three acres or so in a remote area on top of a hill. Some of the money she allowed her sister to use for herself and her children. Ponnamma let her sister handle everything. My mother said that she remembered her father as being very dark in complexion, and that he told stories of the war. My mother remembered his hearty laugh, but when he laughed he would start coughing. A year or so later he succumbed to the T.B, and died. My uncle was too young to remember him at all.

"A couple of years later Ammoomma started her medical practice in Thycaud Hospital, in the town of Trivandrum, and decided to buy her own house in Chenthitta--within walking distance, two blocks from the hospital. She moved her sister, Ponnamma, and the three kids (my mother and her two siblings) with her to the Chenthitta house. The oldest of the brothers was married and working and two of the brothers stayed with him and his wife in the family home. The other sisters lived in the area and kept an eye on them. But Ammoomma decided she could not leave her youngest brother, Dali, and so she took him in, along with her stepmother, into the Chenthitta house. Due to dramatic family events, this is how the new family bonds formed. To my ammoomma we were her immediate family."

Hearing the story, I had a newfound respect that made me adore my ammoomma even more than I already did. Despite my young age I realized how much she loved my aunt, my mother, and my uncle to have taken the responsibility to raise them and adopt them as her own, instead of trying to pursue her own family life. It was noble of her to 'adopt' her sister's children, and kismet because about five years later Ponnamma died from an axillary abscess and septicemia. With both parents deceased, the three siblings would have been orphans had Ammoomma not adopted them and made them her own family.

In my young mind Ammoomma was a queen bee ruling a very organized colony of family members.

My birth mother, Retnamma, was my amma, mother.

Her sister, Saradamma, was older than she by three years. She raised me in my ammoomma's house as my ammachi, and was equally responsible for who I became. I loved them both dearly.

Once I became a mother, I pondered my own upbringing. I understood then why I never felt torn between my two mothers. It was because of the deep love and admiration they had for each other. They adored each other. It was not a daily talked-about, demonstrative hug-and-kiss kind of love. It was how they always looked out for each other's best interests. I could see and feel the sibling love they shared.

My ammachi taught me to read, write, and do my arithmetic. She had unquestioned authority to discipline me. Meanwhile, she could also spoil me with books, new bangles, and fancy clothes whenever she felt like it. My mom never questioned her. Realizing the truth of how different they were in their tastes for books and learning, and in their knowledge of worldly affairs and money matters, I am still surprised that Mom did not argue or protest my ammachi's interest or her influence on me.

My mother did not wish to finish high school, or read literature, or go to the English movies that came to the theatre near us. Ammachi, on the other hand, was earning her masters in Organic Chemistry, and then reading for her doctorate by the time I was six years old. She constantly carried a book in her hand and had piles of magazines by her bedside. Mom would rather chant her prayers or tell us stories of Lord Vishnu saving the world or Goddess Durga slaying the Demon Narakasura. While ammachi read to us from *Readers' Digest*, Mom taught us words to all the prayers she chanted in our pooja room, while we all lived under the same roof with my doctor ammoomma.

Thinking back on that time, I can now feel the way my brain and body absorbed the different blessings from both my mothers. Ammachi and her training cultured a healthy curiosity in me about life outside the Chenthitta House, our hometown, Trivandrum, and our land of India. However, my spiritual side and knowledge were impacted by the pure, ultimate belief in my mother's practice of the Hindu religion and her Hindu practices. My outlook in life developed with a wonderful balance that aided me tremendously when I had to meet life's challenges.

Later, my ammoomma built a separate house for my mom and dad. I remember the *paalu-kaatchu, boiling-the-milk,* ceremony to bless my parents' new home. For the first official entry to their new house, my mom led the way while carrying an oil lamp lit brightly with five wicks. My daddy followed her with a statue of Lord Ganesha, and with great pomp and ceremony the idol was placed in the pooja room, our room for worship. Alongside my parents, my ammachi carried a pot of water used to sanctify the fruit and flowers used for the pooja services. We then proceeded to the kitchen which, of course, was the most important room in the house. A shiny new aluminum saucepan was filled with fresh milk, and placed with reverence over the wood-burning stove. The milk was allowed to boil over as an aus-picious offering to *Bhoomi-Devi*, Goddess Earth. Sugar was added to the boiled milk, which was then offered to Lord Ganesha, to invoke his blessings for their new home. The symbolically blessed milk was then shared with all family members and guests who attended the house-warming function.

Even in her new beginnings, my mom welcomed the full support from her sister, my ammachi.

I, in turn, enjoyed the double mothering bestowed upon me by both.

Ammoomma had chosen to live in the busy area of town because the Women and Children's hospital where she practiced medicine was only half a mile from our house, and she could walk there for deliver-ies, even at night, in a short time. It was close to town and central to all the government offices, various businesses, many of the university colleges, and also to the residential areas. The city bus offered many routes running through the street in front of our house, making it easy for her patients to come see her from all parts of town.

Our street bordered on *Chenthitta Gramam*, or Chenthitta village, a small separate community its own, right in the middle of town. All the families in this village were Brahmins. No other castes owned a house in this *gramam*.

One of my earliest memory is of a young girl named Janaki, whom I called 'Janaki Chechi" (Chechi means older sister), who lived in the gramam. About seven years older than me, she came over and took me to her house and taught me special dances. One such dance was called *kolattam,* where a group of girls danced in rhythm in a circle, and hold fourteen inch-long polished wooden sticks about a half inch in diameter. Each one hit the next girl's stick to make clicking noises to the rhythm of their dance music, as the older girls or the mothers sang songs in praise of Lord Krishna. As they swirled and twisted around in graceful dance moves, their colored skirts twirled around, too, making a magical tableaux right in the middle of the street, which they treated as if it was their front yard anyway. I have been told that Janaki Chechi and her girlfriends called me *"Paapa,"* meaning *'small child'* in *Tamil,* the native language of the Brahmins, and a very ancient Indian language. Our family of Nair caste spoke Malayalam, an old language in itself, but not as old as Tamil. I'd anointed myself with this nickname, *'Paapa,'* when I started talking, and it stuck.

*Chenthitta gramam* consisted of a single street running about two furlongs long, just under half a mile, carrying two rows of houses. At the street level the home-fronts were narrow, the homes going deep and long to the rear. The front entrance of each house had a small veranda in the form of a screened porch, the wooden screens feeble barriers from the street. This led to a front hall which combined a receiving room and an office for the head of the household. There were no front yards. Going farther in, the only source of sunlight was well placed glass roof tiles in each room, between the baked clay roof tiles. As we went deeper, the hallway led to one or two bedrooms, and on to the kitchen, where usually a corner table served as both worktop and dining table. Children slept in the hallways on mattresses which were rolled and put away during the day. Elders had cots in a corner, and these also served as seating when any friend came to visit. Past the kitchen a sunny but small backyard served as a garden and work area. As small as the space might be, a *Tulsi* plant, blue basil, in a pot always took center stage—a holy token to bring blessings on the family. The blue-green leaves from the Tulsi are used in all our pooja rituals.

An open tap provided city water, and a mounted stone was used for washing clothes. Clotheslines carrying the day's laundry made the backyards cluttered and no fun to play in, so children played on the streets. There were not too many cars in those days; the only danger was from the bicycles and the loud clanging of the annoying bicycle-bells.

One constant in each of these homes was a Veena, a stringed instrument with a round resonance box at each end similar to a sitar. The girls took Indian classical music lessons at a very early age. Also present was a violin or trumpet if there was a boy in the house. It was not uncommon for girls to take violin or boys to take Veena, either.

The Brahmins on this street had a very special culture of their own. In addition to their language, they had separate schools where everything was taught in Tamil. They were pure vegetarians and did not even bring eggs into their homes. It was quite a contrast from our home where we had fish and eggs every day and lamb or chicken once in a while.

At the very end of this special street was our temple, where the main deity was Devi, an avatar of Goddess Lekshmi, the goddess of wealth and prosperity. Chenthitta Devi was my main source of inspiration and support when I was growing up. Devi not only brought prosperity, but was very powerful in protecting loved ones, and granting wishes to devotees. Also on the same temple grounds were separate temple sanctums for Lord Ganesha, Lord Krishna, and Lord Shiva.

I practiced special prayers to Ganesha, who eliminated all obstacles, at the start of each school year, prior to term exams, before any special trips we took, or a tennis match.

To Krishna, I made special offerings of flowers and fruit whenever I needed help with matters of the heart. He was, in his avatar on earth, a king of cowherds, and a romantic who was said to have cloned himself into 16,001 Krishnas to dance with thousands of the village maidens in order not to disappoint any of them.

When I attained teenage status I was urged to observe Shiva Vrathams every Monday with a fast dedicated to please Lord Shiva. The one-day fast was to avoid all meats, and start the day with prayers to Lord Shiva. I would attend the evening services at the temple, where I offered flowers and chanted special prayers for Lord Shiva, and then came home to a dinner with rice and vegetable curries, or a light supper with dosas (light flour crepes without eggs). No meat or eggs were allowed. A liquid diet was permitted and all things vegetarian for the whole day.

The Shiva Vratham, or fast for Shiva, had many connotations. In vernacular interpretation, girls and women did this act of religious observance to receive good husbands. A deeper meaning was for the safety and health of the man you loved, your husband or your father/father-figure in your life. A more meaningful aspect to this particular fast was patterned after the longest and hardest fast ever known in our history and mythology, that of Parvathi Devi, who did a rigorous fast for earning Shiva as her husband. The difficulty weighed in on how Lord Shiva stood in a yogic pose, on one leg, atop a Himalayan peak, eyes closed and mind shut off from the rest of the world. To break this intense meditative state and bring him back to living status was by no means a simple task. Parvathi Devi accomplished this by her long fast, undaunted by many obstacles; this is considered the fast to take for a bright future for any girl. After marriage, many women continue the fast, as I do, believing that the health and mental status of the 'man of the house' is most crucial factor in maintaining the stability of any house and home.

To this day, when I sit down in front of the lamp for my Monday prayers, I can see the idol of lord Shiva decorated with flowers and clouded by the smoke of the incense and the camphor cubes lit in devotion for the daily service. I can hear the ringing of the bells, as I ring my own at the conclusion of my prayers, the chiming sounds we send out to carry the prayers to the cosmos and beyond.

Core beliefs, even if they are sometimes blind, have given me inner strength when facing adversities later on in my life. To practice a strong faith and a deep involvement in all matters related to my Hindu religion was a blessing in times of stress. On the flip side, for a long time there were no temples or any other facilities or support systems to help individuals follow the Hindu religious practices in this adopted country of mine.

It was only eighteen years after I came to the US that the first Hindu temple opened its doors in the Chicagoland area. I was very active in the temple services—not only to visit or to pray, but also to help in the evolution of the institution itself. It was gratifying to be able to help organize the initial programs, and I gladly volunteered to help clean the place and to braid floral garlands to be placed on the deities themselves.

Chenthitta Devi Temple, 2017
(With permission from photographer Sankar Narayana)

# 6

## Trains, Trains, and Train-rides.

**I LIVE AN** hour and fifteen minute train ride to downtown Chicago.

Long ago, I rode the train on a regular basis, but later learned the convenience of driving my car also offered the liberty to take detours to-and-from my designated route. Driving also came in handy when Raj's Parkinson's disease made it too difficult to board a train with our satchels and medicines, which included his insulin and the diabetic checking kit.

In recent years, I have gone to Chicago numerous times to attend classes or conferences, and the Metra train schedule has offered a convenient alternative to being stuck in the notoriously slow traffic on the Chicago highways. On the train I sit in comfort to the rocking rhythm that usually puts me to sleep. The clickety-clack transports me back to my history with rail travel when it all began at the end of the line.

My ammoomma's house was across the road from the end of the statewide railroad line—the 'terminus,' I remember being told. As early as 5 o'clock in the morning, we were wakened by the rattling sounds of coal being dumped into the engine. The rumble of the engines starting shook the house, and the sharp whistles pierced our ears. The local farm trucks loaded with grain and vegetables caused commotion during arrival, emptying their loads and exiting, prior to the train leaving for other cities.

Many times we stood on wobbly wooden stools to look over the compound wall separating our yard from the road and view of the railroad. Our small eyes grew round and wide, filled with fascination as we watched the railroad cars switch the tracks while the engine manually turned around on huge rotating platforms. The adults of the house complained of the noise and the traffic, and about the soot soiling  freshly painted outside walls, but we children never tired of the noises, and it excited us every chance we got to see the trains.

Though the train station was close, we did not travel by train too often. My ammoomma did not take public transport by bus or train for any local travels. She did not wish to be in the company of her patients other than when they needed her. She bought a Morris Minor car when I was ten years old, but before this she either went places by taxi cab or used a friend's car. She had enough wealthy friends who were only too glad to send their car and chauffeur for her use. My special train trip came when I was eleven years old. My Aunt Ammachi was to attend an International conference in *Applied Chemistry*  in Calcutta, a main city in Bengal, which was once the capital of India under the British rule. She, with her husband, my *Valiachan,* decided to combine a vacation tour of North India at the same time. They invited Ammoomma to go with them. She in turn told me that if my dad paid for me, I could go with them.

From our home in the far south end of India, we traveled by train to Calcutta in the northeast part of the country. Novel experiences awaited me. I enjoyed my sleep in the top berth of the sleeping coach, and for dinner I ate steaming hot food served on steel trays. It was January and the train felt colder the further north we traveled. My ammachi helped me into the woolen pajamas that had been tailored for my special trip. I wore them under my skirts and wore a warm sweater over my blouse. In Calcutta, I was amazed and intimidated by how crowded the town was. The Hoogly River was even busier than the streets, with the boats and large barges ferrying people and sacks of goods to the River Ganges, as she flowed eastward to the Bay of Bengal. The river mouth had a big, busy port where the ships from all over the world traded for the silk, jute, rice, and spices like cardamom, cloves and cinnamon from all over India. The railroad as well as the waterways fed all the goods to the port.

We visited museums and universities and a hospital ward which was much larger than the ones in the Women and Children's hospital in Thiruananthapuram. Its large size was monumental by comparison, but it was more crowded and less clean. The strong smells of disinfectants and disease made an impression on me. One of the doctors who worked there described the different research projects especially on infectious diseases, I wished more than ever to go study medicine and take care of the sick.

What I remember the most was the Calcutta Botanical Gardens. It was not the large Canna blooms or the brilliant-colored roses that fascinated me. It was the huge Banyan tree that covered a whole four block distance. For over a century, the aerial roots hung down, growing new trees where they reached the ground and stayed connected at the top by the intertwining branches forming a roof of green over a vast area. I was so taken by this I made Valiachan walk, and walk, and walk, the entire area covered by it. Of course it tired me out. He lovingly tolerated his eleven-year-old niece who was truly a daughter to him, and how he enjoyed spoiling me. I basked in the glory of all their love, and, speaking of love, we visited the all-time monument of everlasting love: ***the Taj Mahal.***

Our next trip on the train was a novel experience for me. The weather had turned cold and despite the woolen pants I wore under my skirt, and the sweater and jacket that I wore, I was shivering in the train. At one of the railway stations I saw vendors, mostly young men, who were sitting around hot stoves over pots of boiling tea. My valiachan stepped out and ordered tea for us. The vendors brought the tea to our carriage in clay cups with sugar already added. By the time we finished our tea the train was moving away from the station. After we finished our teas, we tossed the mud cups out the window onto the gravel by the sides of the railroad tracks. When I think of the trip, I still feel the excitement of that young girl and her new experience of disposable teacups. At a different station I ate hot fried snacks called *bhajis.* They were sliced vegetable and green pepper pieces, batter-dipped and fried in oil. They tasted very good, and I stuffed myself on them. Ammoomma warned me to stop eating lest I end up with a bad tummy-ache. I drank more tea and went to sleep full and happy. When I woke, I felt the train slow down again; this time we reached Agra.

My ammachi had already talked to me about the story of Agra. It was a town on the banks of the Yamuna River, where Emperor Shah Jahan had built a monument of love for his beloved wife, Mumtaz Mahal, after she died at the age of thirty-nine in childbirth of her fourteenth child. **The Taj Mahal**, a marble edifice was built over her funeral site in 1662. The white marble exhibited designs of unbelievable beauty done with inlaid stones, jade, carnelian, lapis lazuli, and coral. While the story intrigued me, the beauty enthralled me and the trip excited me, it was not until much later in life when I experienced my own love story that I fully understood the depth of Shah Jahan's feeling for Mumtaz, and could even imagine why he built that monument.

Our next stop was *Varanasi* or Benares, the holy city on the banks of *Ganga*, the river Ganges.

We reached the Shiva temple where the idol of Shiva was made of black stone, and sat on the floor within arms' reach. In the south Indian temples the idols were placed on elevated platforms and mostly in Sanctum Santorum where the priests did pooja. The devotees did not go inside. On the other hand, in Varanasi all visitors reached up to the idol of Lord Shiva to touch and gain blessings. At eleven years of age, this was to me sacrilegious and I was in shock. I started crying and almost ran out of the temple. Valiachan stopped me and Ammachi hugged me and consoled me. My first exposure to a different culture even within our deep culture of Hinduism was not a pleasant one. Finally, I stopped crying and we completed circumambulation around the temple and concluded our prayers. We proceeded to walk down to the River Ganges.

The devout Hindu girl that I was, and a little fanatic, I looked forward to stepping into the holy waters of the River Ganges and procuring my blessings. When we reached the *Ghat*, a passage or flight of steps leading to the water, I was excited and overwhelmed by the vast body of flowing water and immediately sensed the force of its flow. My heart beat fast and, with youthful enthusiasm, I ran down the steps toward the river.

"Stop right there," my ammoomma called after me. "You are not stepping into that dirty water. If you do, I will break your legs." I burst out crying. I had dreamt of my visit into the waters of Holy River Ganges all through my trip, many miles from my hometown, Trivandrum, in South India. But my wise Ammoomma saw how polluted the river was, not only because of industrial pollution, but also due to the Hindu ritual of immersing burning corpses of cremation into the holy river so the souls can attain salvation. (Since then the practice has been curbed, and the river has been cleaned up; so I am told.) In any case, after my ammoomma forbade me from entering the waters, I returned from that trip without the blessings from the holy waters of Maa Ganga. This was a great disappointment for me. My ammachi teased me for many years to follow about how I pouted and carried on until I fell asleep on the train ride from Benares to Bombay, our next destination.

(Later on in my life I did make a trip to the Himalayas where the four main tributaries of the Ganges River originate. My pilgrimage to Maa Ganga is recounted in my last Memoir, ***Song of the Mountains***)

# 4

## Doctors, Mentors, and Momentous Decisions

**FOR MANY YEARS** Ammoomma took Shanthi and me to visit her dear friend, colleague and mentor, Mrs. Ponnen Lukose. She was the Chief Medical Officer of Women and Children's Hospital in Trivandrum at the time.

Dr. Lukose was active in the politics of health care. Having been educated in England, she attended conferences there and in other foreign lands. When she was out of town or busy with meetings, my ammoomma took care of her patients and helped run the hospital with help from other physicians on the staff. The outpatient clinic offered a challenge all its own. There were long lines of patients every day who received checkups and medicines. This was a time before penicillin, so people's streptococcal infections with rheumatic fever as well as kidney disease wreaked havoc in the population they served. In addition, the obstetrics department was very busy as well. Ammoomma was known for her magic fingers that helped difficult pregnancies pull through, yielding a healthy baby and healthy mother. It didn't matter whether the delivery involved forceps or a Caesarian section, Ammoomma could do it all.

Often Dr. Lukose, whom I called doctor-amma, would stop by

the house to talk with Ammoomma about their patients or about an upcoming surgical procedure. As a child I sat on Dr. Lukose's lap and played with her long gold chain. It was a classic 'muthumala,' two strands of small gold balls, united at the top with a gold bar about half inch long. My ammoomma also wore a similar chain. The word muthu means 'drop,' and the golden balls are considered golden drops.

As they finished their discussions, I would get off of doctor-amma's lap, gather her black medical bag and stethoscope, and with reverence I would hand them to her. She would run her fingers through my curls and kiss the top of my head before saying goodbye to my ammoomma.

Later, I learned that my doctor-amma was the Surgeon General of our State of Kerala, and she would later become the Surgeon General of the nation. She was the first ever woman Surgeon-General in the world.

When I was eight I went with Ammoomma to visit Dr. Mary Ponnen Lukose on Christmas day. We had slices of black halva, made with a special kind of rice flour, simmered long with coconut milk, butter and brown sugar until it solidifies. Slivers of almonds and cardamom flavor it, and once cooled it's cut up into squares like brownies, except the pieces are moist and wiggly even after they are sliced. Dr. Lukose told me I needed to come back the next week because Grace Chechi, her daughter, who was a professor at Lady Hardinge Medical College and Hospital in Delhi, would be coming home to visit for a month. I returned with my ammoomma the next week to see Grace Chechi, who was much older than me. She was tall, with broad shoulders, and had a stately gait; she could be quite intimidating. I was in awe of her knowledge, and all the information she revealed about her medical school in the faraway place of New Delhi. I was also impressed by the fact that she was a professor at Lady Hardinge Medical School. Yet, once she smiled her broad open smile, her face wrinkled up around her dark brown eyes and I felt at ease listening to her. When she sat down and played the piano for my ammoomma and her mother, I sat on a soft, cushy chair while I ate the soft halva served to me on a plate with a short silver fork. I was happy dreaming of one day becoming an accomplished doctor.

A week after my visit, my dad drove to the Holy Angels' Convent school to pick up my sister and me. Once we were in the car he broke the news to us that Grace-Chechi had an accident and died suddenly. I could not believe it. He drove us directly to doctor-amma's house. Grace, the vibrant young doctor, was laid in the front hall, surrounded by white roses. By her feet, a brass oil lamp was lit.

Wailing relatives and friends lined the walls of the large room, followed by dignitaries such as ministers and judges and other physicians. Another stream of family and friends flowed through the large room to say goodbye much like the first wave. I was in shock, and both Shanthi and I were sobbing so hard that Dad decided to take us home after a little while. He returned to the Lukose house later to accompany my ammoomma to the funeral.

Doctor-amma went on to live a very productive life as the national Surgeon General. My last visit with her would be in 1971. I was thirty-one years old. She ran her fingers through my curls again right before I left, just as she had done all through my childhood.

Throughout my childhood and youth, she was but a doctor and Ammoomma's friend; but when I found out all that she accomplished in her lifetime, I was awed and proud to have had the privilege of knowing her so intimately. I was unaware then of how important a part my ammoomma and Doctor Amma, (Dr. Mrs. Ponnen Lukose,) played in my decision to pursue a career in medicine.

There was one other close friend of my ammoomma who was a constant in my childhood. This was Dr. K.P. Janaki. She also graduated from Vellore Medical College. They visited each other often. I loved listening to them talk shop. No patient detail was beyond my interest. An open book in hand, I sat within earshot of their conversation, and even though I understood nothing beyond the fact that the patient got better, I listened earnestly to every word they spoke. Theirs was a world of wonder, glamor and hope to which I dreamed of belonging— and one into which I jumped both feet first at the initial opportunity.

1939, Dad and Mom

1943, Mom, Shanthi, Shaku, Dad.

# 8

## The Onam Festival

**NEW YEAR'S DAY,** Chingam 1st, 1116, on the Dravidian calendar that is followed in Kerala, fell in the middle of August, 1940 on the Gregorian calendar.

My mother was eight months pregnant with her first child who turned out to be me. The first day of the year is always special. But that particular year close relatives and my ammoomma outdid themselves making my mom's favorite foods, making sure she did not have to do many of her usual chores, and helping her with anything she had to do. Retnamma, my mother, was the sweetest person you could know. She had just turned nineteen that June and being that she was carrying the oldest grandchild of Doctor Chellamma, and the first child of photographer Sivaraam, she was all but placed on a pedestal and well catered to.

The most rewarding part of being a child in Thiruananthapuram in the '40s was how simple life was. The festivals that dotted every month of the year made it a yearlong celebration of life. The very word 'festival,' summons up scenes of vivacity and partying.

Festivals formed an integral part of being an Indian. When all stories were told, I came to realize how the festivals were as varied as the people and their religions. Even at six years of age, I recognized how festivals vary in different regions of the country. But there was one common element whether you were at the Northern State of Uttarkhand or the Southern State of Kerala where I grew up: Every occasion called for family rejoicings and feasting. Not that we needed any excuse to gather and share food, family stories and laughs.

Most Indian festivals exercise their origin in religion or in the myths and legends which are very central in the lives of an Indian. Whatever the reason may be, as a child I longed for these occasions with great anticipation and excitement--for the people, the food, the gifts and the fiesta.

In our family, the Onam festival marked the ultimate in celebrations. It began in the first month of the Malayalam calendar, *Chingam*. One can liken **the Onam festival** to the Christmas season, but with more family interaction involving fun with their community, Indian food, gifts and the fiesta while the schools are on vacation for two weeks. People of all religions, castes and communities celebrate the festival with equal joy and verve. Onam also helps to create an atmosphere of peace and brotherhood by way of various organized sports during the ten days of the festival. (Onam is not only the biggest festival of Kerala by any standard, but also one that has been a part of the Malayalee psyche for centuries. The earliest record of the festival is found during the reign of **Kulasekhara Perumals**, the rulers of the land, around AD 800. Onam reflects the faith of the people of Kerala: a belief in their legendary past, religion and power of worship. Onam is also a harvest festival. It is celebrated at a time when the bounty of nature is at its fullest. The beautiful landscape of Kerala can be seen in its full radiance at this time of the Malayalam New Year. My ammo-omma's love for me shone brightest at **the Onam festival**, our special annual holiday affair, dedicated to a utopian era when our people were a happy lot under the rule of King Mahabali. Based on this story of the greatest king of all, the Onam festival is Kerala's greatest and happiest celebration. Onam is celebrated in the month of **Chingam**, which falls from the middle of August to the middle of September. It is the first month of our Dravidian calendar and also marks the harvest season. At this time the countryside is at its most enchanting. The torrential rains of the monsoons are over, and the land is lush and full of fragrant flowers. The first harvest of the year lies freshly gathered, so all mankind is moved to celebrate the bounty of nature. As long as I can remember, there has always been a full moon, on or within two days of the Onam day. One of the most marvelous facets of Onam is the unfolding of its rich and well-established culture. We see not just glimpses of the culture, but a whole gamut of it in the ten-day-long carnival where classical and folk dancers perform in secular fabric, boat races are conducted, and parades of people with groups performing tiger dances, pass through the streets in many towns. Various folk arts and crafts are highlighted by the roadside and are honored and celebrated.

Every year, the aunts and uncles, cousins and in-laws, all came to celebrate Onam with us at my ammoomma's house, because she was the matriarch.

Preparations for the festival started early. For ten days before the main festival day, called Thiruonam, or sacred Onam, a floral decoration is done each morning in the front yard. This is called *Athapoovu*, a circular design of fresh flowers, with various vibrant colors making a strong statement of welcome to our legendary, mythical King Mahabali, who comes to visit the land and his people at this time.

My sisters and I, with the help of my cousin, scoured our neighborhood for the best blooms for our floral patterns. We have some fun stories of how we stole ready-to-bloom buds of the brightest yellow flowers from the gardens at the college campus where my aunt worked. We did not get caught because the gardener himself helped to bend the boughs in order for our young limbs to reach the buds. We brought them home and placed them in a shallow pan of clay with wet rags over them so they would not wilt before blooming the next morning. The reddest red in the design came from the hibiscus in my aunt's garden. My mother provided the rose petals from her rose garden. We were guided by the older cousins to keep the patterns circular and to keep the mess to a minimum. Separating petals from the larger blooms and keeping color combinations unadulterated were not easy for six- and eight-year-old hands. The pungent smells of marigolds, the bitter-sweet aroma of the oleanders, the sweet smells of two or more variety of jasmines, intermingled with the divine smell of the special pink rose, *the panineer-poovu,* from which the best rose-essence is made.

1949. The floral design of **Athapoovu** in my mother's front yard.
Shaku, Hari, Jayee and Shanthi,

During the main day of Onam, termed *Thiruonam,* it was customary for the head of the family to give new clothes to children in the family. I remember when I was six I received the best outfit from my ammoomma.

I sat and listened to my father tell the story of King Mahabali (fondly called *Maveli*) as he did every year. Decked in our new outfits, the children, along with most of the adults, gathered around him to hear the story of Onam.

"Our land of Kerala is green, lush, and beautiful, warm and inviting, nestled between the Sahya Mountains to the east and the Arabian Sea to the west. Long, long ago, when King Maveli ruled, the land was true utopia," my father said in his full, expressive voice, and unforgettable narrative flair.

He then broke out into a famous song about King Maveli.

> *"Maveli naadu vaanidum kaalam*
> *Maanusharellarum onnu pole*
> *aamodathode vasikkum kaalum*
> *Apathangarkum ottilla thanum*
> *Kallavum illa chathiyum illa*
> *Kollatharangal mattoonum illa."*

"When Maveli ruled the Land, all men were equal.
They lived happily and they were threatened by none.
There was no dishonesty, no cheating, and no acts of violence in the land,"
He explained for further emphasis.

"You see môl, back then; peace, prosperity, and goodwill were the rules of the land. King Maveli was generous to a fault. His people followed suit."

"How come nobody was bad?" I questioned.

"When each and every person had a job and made enough money to provide food, clothes, and all comforts to his family," father replied, "there was no need to steal from another."

He went on to explain how this state of bliss created a problem for the *devas*, the gods in heaven. They were afraid that when a true utopia existed on earth, the people would not have any use for the *devas* or their heavenly blessings.

"They, the *devas*, begged Lord Vishnu, the Sustainer of the Universe, to please curb Maveli's power. Lord Vishnu appeared before the King as Vamana, a dwarf, and asked for a plot of land, to be measured by three footsteps for prayers and penance. The generous king readily agreed. Suddenly Vamana took his cosmic, gigantic form." Here, my father got off his easy-chair, and for effect, stood tall with his hairy chest fully expanded, as he continued the story.

My younger sister, Shanthi, grabbed my arm; she was so engrossed in our father's narration.

"In two huge strides Vamana covered the earth and heaven. For the third stride, he demanded more space. Maveli bowed down and offered his head." Father lifted his foot and stomped hard on the floor, even as he spoke. "Vamana placed his foot on Maveli's head and pushed the king out of his earthly kingdom."

Shanthi tightened her grip on me.

Father was silent for a full minute, letting the event sink in. Then he spoke, softly and deferentially, in a tone and cadence akin to saying a prayer.

"The King's people prayed to Lord Vishnu that once a year he be allowed to visit his beloved subjects. The Lord granted their wish and since then King Maveli comes to Kerala to visit his people once a year, on Onam day."

Father sat down, and took Shanthi on his lap.

He resumed his upbeat story-teller tone, and continued. "Our families gather and recreate the spirit of the utopia that we lost a long time ago."

I saw Ammoomma smile at his dramatics as he entertained us all with his Onam story.

On the tenth day we partook in an elaborate Onam lunch, called the Ona-Sadya, in which the items served were quite specific and the presentation very ritualistic. The seven-course Sadya was served on fresh-cut banana palms, the pointed end facing to my left. Three different hot and spicy pickles, ginger, lemon and mango, were artistically placed in a fanned-out manner, on the outer edges of each banana leaf. Customarily, four vegetables dishes, one aviyal, a mixed vegetable dish, two, thoran, a chopped vegetable dish with grated coconut, cumin, and garlic flavors, three, olan, a bean and squash dish with milk in the gravy, and a cucumber and yogurt kichadi were served. No meat was ever served at an Ona-Sadya.

For the first course, warm mounds of rice were placed on the banana leaves and parippu, cooked dhal sauce, poured over the rice. Spoonfuls of ghee, clarified butter, were layered over this, and thus started the Ona-sadya. The second course was the spicy sambar ladled generously over more steamed rice.

The third course, and the highlight of the Ona-sadya, was the ada-payasam, a porridge-like dessert of rice noodles, simmered long and slow in coconut milk and brown sugar, and laced with a touch of cardamom. It is truly divine and helped to soothe my mouth, still burning from the chili peppers in the sambar.

A second payasam of rice, milk, and sugar paal-payasam followed.

After this sweet break came more rice and the last three courses: pulisseri, rasam, and moru, a diluted yogurt sauce flavored with curry leaves and green pepper.

To supplement all this flavor we were also served small sweet bananas, and pappadums, fried wafers made from urad dhal, and vattal, green banana chips. What I liked best were upperis, made of chunks of fried green bananas coated generously in melted brown sugar spiced with crushed ginger and cardamom, giving an exotic feel to your palette.

The Onam feast was the ultimate standard by which all other happenings in life were measured. If one made a windfall profit in business, we said, "Onam vannallo," meaning onam has come for you. If we acted too cocky, we were told we had to eat "a few more ona-sadyas" to qualify for whatever opinion we were presumptuous about. If one acted too young or immature, we were told, 'You have passed too many Onams to act this silly.'

As the matriarch, my ammoomma was always the first one to be served the Ona-Sadya. She insisted that we, her grandchildren, be served alongside of her. I sat to her right. We sat on the floor upon hand-woven mats of dried grass stalks, dyed in colorful designs, as we shared the most special feast, Ona-Sadya, with my ammoomma on the most special day of the year. Little did I know that our Onam together in 1957 would be the last year that I would have the privilege of being her special young one who sat by her right side for the Ona-sadya. The next year, as a medical student, I would be elevated to the adult status, my younger siblings taking my place beside my ammoomma.

One vast difference between the Onam celebrations and Christmas celebration was that *Maveli's* visit was celebrated as a community affair more than just in the family setting.

After the feast, in many families women gathered and performed **Kaikottikali,** or **Thiruvathirakali,** a group dance where both young and old submerge themselves in the spirit of the occasion and dance with perfect ease. They wear a gold-bordered traditional two piece cloth called mundu and neriyathu. A mundu is a one-piece cloth draped on the lower part of the body while neriyathu is worn over a blouse.

Usually eight to ten dancers move in circles, sometimes in clockwise and sometimes in anti-clockwise direction, gracefully bending in sideways as they do so. They also beautifully coordinate their hand movements as they go, clapping upwards and downwards in rhythm with the beat and in tune with the song they are following.

In other places, men participated in a strenuous form of contact sport, the kalaripayattu, a form of martial arts dating back to the Sangam literature of about the 3rd century BC to the 2nd century where these techniques were part of the training for fighting and defense among troops of the kingdom.

### Kaduvakali

On the fourth day of Onam, people celebrate the Pulikali Play, also called Kaduvakali. To perform in the play groups, local men get their bodies and faces painted to resemble tigers. The theme of the performance is playing hide-and-seek with a hunter holding a gun. The event generates a great deal of excitement both for the spectators from near and far and for the performers.

**Boat races**. They also have boat races in the various canals and lagoons of Kerala. The most famous boat race is the one held at Alleppy. The races are held in long snake-like boats called **chundans**, each being rowed by nearly a hundred men, singing songs in a very spirited fashion.

Kathakali

Kathakali, performances (story-plays of Indian epics) are held at various forums such as the Victoria Jubilee Town Hall in Trivandrum. These started at 10:00 p.m, and concluded at pre-dawn.

What I remember best was that my ammoomma let us skip school the next day so we could catch up on our sleep. She was confident that our experience attending the performances afforded more education and wisdom to us than any school books could provide.

When I married Raj in January 1963, I had to leave my ammoomma's home and move to Raj's home with my mother-in-law and Raj's siblings. It was normal and expected. We girls grew up knowing our place was in our husband's home after we married. Six months after our wedding, Raj left for Chicago for higher studies. I still had to complete my rotating internship before I could graduate medical school and join Raj in Chicago. Meanwhile I continued to live with Thankom Maami, my mother-in-law, and seven of Raj's siblings, ranging from three years of age to fifteen years. Thankom Maami was widowed for two and a half years, and she would be celebrating Onam without Raj, her first-born, for the first time in her life, so I stayed on for the Ona-sadya with her. Although I visited my ammoomma later in the day, I had missed the magic of our Ona-sadya with her and my daddy. I was a grown-up belonging to a different family by marriage and commitment. Neither my ammoomma nor my dad let on as to how much they missed me for their ona-sadya. But I knew within my heart that my ammoomma wanted me by her right side as she sat down for her ona-sadya, as much as I wanted to be there. But duty and commitments were honored at all cost. That separation at Onam gave me a foreboding of what would happen when I moved away to Chicago, too far away to even think about returning for an Onam celebration with my Ammoomma.

My first Onam in Chicago, in 1964, without my ammoomma, Dad, Mom, and Thankom Maami or all the rest of the family was very hard because I could not accept the fact that I would not be sharing the ada-payasam, and that I would not have a real Ona-sadya with the family I left behind. For that matter it was hard on my friend Padma too. She also had traveled here with her husband the same year.

The two of us, along with a few other friends, tried to recreate our Onam. I was six months pregnant and Padma was four months pregnant. We laughed and cried at the challenges in front of us. In 1964 the stores did not carry eggplant or okra all the time. Those were the key vegetables for our Sambar, and without them our Sambar did not taste the same. We made it anyway. For the dish called *parippu*, made of skinned, split peas from the green *moong dhal,* we had to order it from New York. Fortunately, our order came in time for our Onam feast. The classic Ona-Sadya required a sweet dessert called payasam made of flat rice noodles called ada, and we did not have rice flour to make it with that year. I remember the year after that we pre-ordered and saved rice flour in time to make ada-payasam for Onam in 1965. That year we made a payasam with noodles and sugar and condensed milk. So sweet and tasty, it made up for some of the missing ingredients.

Thus we managed the best we could. We gathered as many of our friends as we could, (some of the doctors were invariably on call at the hospital), and served our version of the Ona Sadya. The highlight of the day was our stories of Onam. We laughed hilariously as we told of the different types of rope-swings, and the time one or more fell off the swing because it was swung too high or because they stood up on the swings and did acrobatics.

It was not quite the same, but the spirit of Onam did raise our spirits and definitely helped overcome other challenges we faced.

I learned then that the love of family ingrained in me as a child gave me a sense of confidence. It was not the daily ingredients of life but the deep faith in myself that helped me overcome obstacles and continues to take me to the heights of satisfaction in whatever I accomplish.

Onam was and remains a renewal of that self where utopia is what you make within you at any junction in life. Maveli's Utopia is there whenever you close your eyes and choose to be in it.

Later, in the '70s and '80s, Indian grocery stores popped up in the Chicagoland area, and I learned where to search and find Spanish grocery stores that carried some of our vegetables such as yucca and yam. A few years down the line when the next generation of Indians immigrated to the States, more of the familiar items were imported from South and Central Americas and our way of crafting authentic south Indian dishes became easier. This made me happiest at Onam time when the prescribed courses of dishes were most important to me. I also have gained the wisdom to appreciate things in life more and more as I grow older because I learned how difficult it was to do without what I truly love.

# 9

## *Saraswathi Pooja*

**THE SECOND MONTH** of our Malayalam calendar year is *Kanni,* which starts in the middle of September and goes to the middle of October. This was always a special month for me because I was born on 16th of Kanni which fell in the beginning of October.

According to Indian astronomy, wherein our beliefs are deeply rooted, twenty-eight main stars rule the days of the month and our lives are influenced by the daily rotation of the stars. The star *Atham* dominated the sky on the day, the hour, and to the minute when I was born. I am said to have been 'born under *Atham* star.' An astronomer then calculated the rotation of the earth and the planets and the re-lationship of my star to the nine main planets and drew up a chart, which is the basis of my personal horoscope.

Each year my birthday is celebrated on the date the *Atham* star comes to shine on the earth according to our Malayalam calendar. This date fell on different dates in the Gregorian calendar. Since my mother and aunt kept track of such dates, they reminded us when our birth-days fell.

Early in the morning on my star birthday, I took a bath, donned new clothes and went to the temple with my amma. When I came home from school, a special sweet treat called *payasam* awaited me. Ammachi knew I loved ada-payasam: rice noodles simmered long and slow with butter, brown sugar and coconut milk, and then flavored with crushed cardamom and sliced bits of coconut, browned lightly in melted butter. We did not hold birthday parties after the first three or four years of a child's life. Now children's birthday parties with birthday cakes are the norm of the day. Not everybody brought us birthday presents. I felt very blessed and cherished by all the attention I received.

One year Dad went to Madras for an *Agfa* photography convention. He happened to return a few days before my seventh birthday and he brought me silk material for a blouse to go with my long skirts. Of course the tailor had to stitch the blouse before my birthday because that was one day I could skip wearing the plain school uniform I had to wear every day to school. I felt like a princess in my blouse made of pure red silk with gold thread woven crisscross, forming small square designs all over it. The blouse came down midway between my hips and my knees and lay over a form-fitted, white satin skirt on my seven-year-old body. I will never forget how special I felt.

What I do remember is something I really don't want to remember.

We had a *dhobi*, a lady who took all our clothes to wash and iron and returned them two days later. With special instructions and the gentle "Lux" brand soap (provided by Ammachi), she was very dependable and treated all our clothes very well. My special blouse was also sent out with her. Two days later as I stood by the wall that separated the Chenthitta house from the main road in the front, (we did this to pass time and to see the traffic go by) I saw the dhobi's daughter, about my age on her way to the temple, wearing my shiny red silk blouse. I was in tears, and my ammachi came running. She too saw the blouse. I was inconsolable. Ammachi promised to get it back for me and assured me it would be rewashed and ironed.

I did get it back and it was in good condition but the magic was gone. It was just another blouse to me after that. I was glad when I grew out of it.

Thinking back, I am surprised I was upset about it because I'd learned to share my belongings and grew up not being possessive of things. I must have been too young to understand, but it was the idea that my dad had brought it for me on a special occasion.

The main festival in the month of **Kanni** is **Navarathri,** or the festival of nine nights. This is in honor of **Devi**, Goddess, in *different* manifestations in which she has appeared on earth to help preserve peace and stability by conquering evil on earth.

In the first three days and nights of Navarathri, we do Pooja services to *Durga,* the goddess who is the embodiment of strength and courage. The next three nights we invoke the blessings of *Lekshmi,* the goddess of wealth and prosperity. The last three nights are dedicated to prayers of *Saraswathi,* the goddess of learning and knowledge. On the tenth day, called *Vijayadasami*, or the victorious tenth day, we conclude the prayers with invoking the blessings of Saraswathi Devi.

Each year Shanthi and I helped Ammachi and Amma set up a special altar and placed a painting of Saraswathi Devi for the Navarathri pooja. Devi was depicted wearing a white and gold saree, holding a Veena, musical instrument with resonance bowls at each end and four strings along its length. In her right palm she held a book representing Vedic knowledge and in her left a string of flowers. A peacock sat beside her as her transport.

We placed flower-garlands strung with aromatic jasmines or chrysanthemums on her, and lit an oil lamp. In front of her we placed all items needed for our education: our class books, the Bhagavat Gita, and any special reading material we liked. Tennis racquets, musical instruments as Veena, violin, guitar, or flute, any item that one of us was training on were placed by the altar to be blessed by Saraswathi Devi. In our home a stethoscope and medical books were also included. For the last forty-eight hours of the festival, the oil lamp stayed lit by the altar without a break. I remember being in charge of watching the level of the oil so it got replenished as needed to keep the flame from going out. Seeing my books, tennis racquet and school items displayed on the special altar to be blessed gave me a newly found confidence that what I was learning at school would be beneficial and my studies fruitful.

Every morning and at dusk, special food items such as: flavored chickpeas called *chundal*, sweet rice payasam called *aravana,* and also bananas and mangos and fresh flowers were offered at the altar to propitiate the Goddess.

The schools honored the occasion with three days of holidays to enable the books to be blessed at the altar. On the morning of *Vijayadasami*, we had a special *aarti,* including the burning of incense and waving lit camphor at the altar to invoke Saraswathi's blessing on all our objects of learning and on all the students in the house. Any arts and crafts we did were blessed also. In our house we never stopped learning, whether it was for making a livelihood or for having fun. Even the carom-board game which required learned skills had to be blessed.

At the conclusion of the Pooja, we did a special ritual to rededicate ourselves to continue our learning process.

A layer of rice grain is spread on a silver tray, and using a piece of dried turmeric root about an inch long for a stylus, each of us wrote "ॐ," Ohm, followed by **Hari Shree Ganapathaye Namah**, an invocation to lord Ganapathi, the elephant-headed God who gets rid of obstacles. We wrote all this in Malayalam alphabet, our native language. As a symbol of re-dedication to our learning, each of us scribed the entire Malayalam alphabet on a layer of rice grain. We followed this by writing the English alphabet. In conclusion whoever took music lessons played their instruments. This was "*Vidhyarambam.*" It means beginning of an education, or re-starting the learning process all over again.

Annually this is the blessed time when two-year-olds are first taught to write. When Jayee, my younger sister, was two years old, I remember her initiation to writing. My dad sat in front of the altar and, holding Jayee's right hand within his palm, he guided her fingers to write "ॐ" on the layer of rice grain. Rice being the staple food in our land, this was an auspicious beginning for her education.

Once all the children participated in the re-dedication, we were allowed to partake of the blessed food from the Pooja. This was the climax and the fun part for us as children.

This season held another special treat for us because of where we lived. The *Brahmins* were a caste of people among Hindus who were priests and teachers and who specialized in the learning of the sacred Vedas and chanting of the Sanskrit texts across generations. They lived in the street on my way to the Chenthitta Devi Temple. They had a unique altar set up for Navarathri called '*Bhamma Kolu*' for this particular pooja season. In each of their houses seven steps were made and all ten *avatars* of Lord Vishnu were displayed in small clay figurines. Also placed on the steps were human figures representing the entire workforce in the region. Farmers with their oxen in front of them as they tilled their rice fields, carpenters with their arms raised with hammers over nails on wooden boards, miniature coconut palms with workers ready to climb them, and boats showing vegetables and grains and some boats even holding bundles of *coir*, loaded for transport.

Painted clay figures of a young girl playing the Veena, children reading books, ladies singing, dancers in classical Indian dance outfits, all these were placed on the steps too. The *Bhomma- Kolu* represented the Divinity we prayed to and our lifestyle in a miniature universe.

Every evening for nine days we were invited to their homes. It was like the modern day open house. The only requirement was the children visiting had to sit in front of the oil lamp lit as part of the Bhomma Kolu and sing a prayer before they were given any of the special treats piled up on brass trays. Shanthi and I had no problem singing or chanting our prayers. Usually our friends in the home we were visiting joined us in the chanting.

At the end of our chanting, our reward came in different forms. Sometimes we were given spicy *bondas* to eat, potato balls dipped in chick pea batter and deep fried. Muruku, are also deep fried, and are not-too-spicy crunchies with rice flour. Then there were sweet, sweet jilebis. Jilebis are made with urad grain flour mixed with some wheat flour, and fried in thin, pretzel-shaped forms and soaked in sugar syrup flavored with saffron. Whatever the snacks, we loved to taste them because they were always different from what we ate at home.

After the summer heat of March, April, and May, the monsoons in June and July cooled off the air, and August still remained warm but enjoyable. In September-October, *Kanni veyil*, or the sunshine of Kanni, carried hot winds from the East which did not bear any moisture. If the temperatures were to stay high, the schools that had no air conditioning closed for a week or so.

One such year, when I was nine years old, my ammoomma took Shanthi, myself, and three cousins, to a hill station where the waterfalls of Courtallam were. Ammoomma did not own a car. Mr. Annachi, a businessman in town whose entire family was Ammoomma's patients, sent his car for our use. Ammoomma's friend, Dr. Janaki, also came with us. About an hour out of Trivandrum, the cool winds from the mountains were a welcome change already. With the bananas, peanuts and cookies at hand we were not complaining even when it was hot. Ammoomma insisted we play word-games or sing songs on the trip. We took turns singing cinema melodies and chanting our prayer songs. We were also encouraged to make up short stories.

The sun was fast approaching the horizon, and Ammoomma asked the driver how much farther we had to go. He answered that it would probably take another hour. He also told Ammoomma that Annachi had arranged two rooms at the rest house and ordered supper for us. Ammoomma was very pleased.

All of a sudden the traffic ahead of us slowed down. Farther ahead we saw a crowd of people at the side of the road, so our driver pulled over and stepped out of the car to find out what was going on. Upon his return, he approached Ammoomma's window and whispered something. We saw her smile and a minute later said, "All right, children, there is a python above us. You may get out if you want to see him."

We trooped out of the car quietly, and joined the hushed crowd. We held hands for moral support. Looking up we saw large green trees lining both sides of the road. At the very top the long branches almost touched each other over the center of the road. The crowd gathered by the roadside pointed to a tree ahead of us and there it was. A full grown python was twisted and curled around a long branch of one tree and a quarter of his length was extended over the road and rested gracefully looped over the top of the tree from the opposite side of the road. It was a scary sight. This python was longer and thicker than the one we had seen in the reptile house at the Thiruananthapuram Zoo.

A man at the scene, who watched this drama for over half hour, said that the python was asleep. If it ate a good meal it would sleep for at least six hours, sometimes eight hours. We stood watching, our mouths agape. Finally Ammoomma said we had to get going. So, under protest, we piled back into the car.

When we arrived at Courtallam, we walked to our rooms and unpacked our stuff. Three of us in one bed in Ammoomma's room, and two on the second bed in Dr. Janaki's room.

We ate supper in the dining hall downstairs where it was a very simple unadorned room with half a dozen tables, and two benches to each table. We ate *Poories* with *potato masala*. Poories are made of whole wheat flour formed into dough and adding salt and melted butter. Then they are rolled into small balls, then rolled flat into circles. They are deep fried in simmering hot oil and drained in a colander to get rid of some of the oil. *Potato masala* are cubed, cooked potatoes, garnished with mustard seeds, onions, red and green peppers and flavored with turmeric, ginger, cinnamon and cardamom powders. If we ate well, we usually ate one last poori with sugar sprinkled on it. That was quite a treat.

The next morning we drove to the waterfalls. There are many different falls that together form the Courtallam Waterfalls. A bridge and a walkway are present in front of the largest of the falls. I still can't believe our Ammoomma let us walk under the falls where we got totally soaked. Perhaps she let us explore since Mr. Annachi had arranged a tour guide to help us walk along the slippery walkway under the falls. Finally, Ammoomma herded us back to our rooms to dry up and change out of our wet clothes. Ammachi had packed the light cotton towels, which came in handy. She helped us to towel-dry our hair, and the older cousins helped the younger ones to dress. When all of us were ready we went to lunch at an outside café. Ammoomma even let us drink hot coffee to warm us up.

I can close my eyes and still feel the delight of the unusual experiences.

I experienced a different side to Ammoomma during this trip. Ammoomma was so gentle and kind—out of character from the strict matriarch at home. I gained great insight from her attitude of exposing us to the various encounters which helped build confidence in us. I know that type of open-hearted and generous sharing of oneself helped form my character, and it built qualities in me that made me successful and content in my adult interactions and my life.

# 10

## *Diwali or Deepavali*

**IT WAS STILL** dark outside when my mother gently shook me awake. I did not want to wake up until she said, "It is ***Diwali*** today. We have to get to the temple." I crawled out of bed, my eyes still half closed as she led me around the back of the house and to the corridor toward the bathroom. She sat me on the parapet wall on the side of the corridor and said, "Don't fall off. Okay?"

She then rubbed warm coconut oil into my scalp. I could smell the black peppercorns in that oil. To prepare the coconut oil used to make our skin and scalp healthy, black peppercorns are fried in the oil, and then sieved out through muslin cloth. The cleared oil is then bottled, and used for our oil bath. She tenderly massaged the oil all over my seven year old body and all over my head. While she let the oil do its magic on me, she brought my toothbrush and paste so I could brush my teeth. I walked over to the bathroom where warm water await-ed me in a big brass pot. My hair was washed with shampoo made from crushed leaves of hibiscus plant and my body was scrubbed with ground *moong dhal* paste. I did not particularly like the slimy feel of the hibiscus leaves, but I liked the moong dhal paste with its pleas-ant smell. The warm water over me felt great. Now I was completely awake. I did not know then that the stuff used on my body was healthy and ecologically harmless. The hibiscus as well as the *moong dhal,* which came from dried green peas, were homegrown, and had no added chemicals.

After drying off with our usual linen-cotton towels, which were thin and easily dried in the sun, I changed into a freshly laundered skirt and blouse. Kamalakshi Chechi brought me a hot cup of coffee. Actually it had more milk than water and was barely flavored with coffee. I enjoyed it immensely, especially since it had sugar added. That was a special treat for having to get up at 4:00 a.m. By the time I finished my coffee, Shanti, my five-year-old sister joined me. She got milk to drink, but no coffee. She was too young. I felt all grown up.

My dad and my uncle were readying the sparklers and the firecrackers in our front yard. At **Diwali,** also called **Deepavali**, the festival of lights, the celebrations differ in different regions of the land.

In North India, we celebrate the victory of King Rama over the demon king Ravana in the epic story of *Ramayana*. The ten-headed demon king, Ravana, kidnaps King Rama's Queen Sita. There ensues a war to rescue her. Ravana is vanquished by Rama, who is the incarnation of Lord Vishnu on this earth with a mission to destroy evil in the land. This time the evil was in Ravana. When Lord Rama returns to his kingdom of Ayodhya with his wife, Sita, there is great celebration in the land and people come out to welcome them. This is the occasion that is celebrated in North India at the Diwali Festival, and the statues of Lord Rama and Sita are carried in procession with people singing and dancing on the streets for miles on end. At the town squares crowds gather to burn the demon, King Ravana's, form in effigy.

Diwali is also associated with bright lights, decorating houses, colourful rangolis, smiling children, beautifully dressed families, mouth-watering delicacies, sweets and lots of happiness. The day is celebrated in honour of Lord Rama (the incarnation of Lord Vishnu in human form) who returned to his kingdom, Ayodhya, after an exile of fourteen long years followed by his coronation. According to the Hindu mythology, everyone in his kingdom cleaned and decorated houses with tiny oil lamps. The name *Deepavali* means 'a row or a series of lights'.

In South India a different victory by Lord Krishna over the demon Narakasura is celebrated at Diwali. To counter the protective Boone given to Narakasura by Lord Shiva, Lord Krishna orchestrates the conflict so that the arrow from his consort, Satyabhama, ends up killing the demon.

Whatever the legend, it is usually a win of good against evil, and the saving of the people on earth from destructive forces.

Through the interaction and the storytelling, we children always got the message of courage, fighting to conquer evil, and the fact that we were descendants of great and divine beings was reiterated at any chance. Even when we were too young to grasp all of it, we understood enough to gather with family and rejoice the win of good versus evil.

We celebrated both occasions together with fireworks before sunrise.

Mom explained to Dad that she would watch the fireworks through the window with Jayee, my two-year-old younger sister, because the flashes of light as well as the noise would scare the baby.

I was allowed to hold the sparklers since I had just turned seven years old. Some of the sparks hit my arms but they were not hot, and they did not burn me. It was more like a tickling feeling. My ammachi helped Shanthi with holding the sparklers to keep her from dropping them and to keep us safe from their hot burning tips. Dad, my uncle, and my cousin set off the larger fireworks. They were loud, bright, and shot orange and blue flames that mesmerized me. There was one that looked like a seven or eight inch stick that my uncle put into the soil, and using a lit sparkler to light its wick, he ran far away to the safety of the verandah where he had already herded us. It took a few seconds to warm up, and with a screeching noise and a shrill whistle, it spewed blue and white flames taller than I for quite a while. I held on fast to my ammachi and I could feel my heart beating fast. There were other firecrackers that shot balls of fire high into the air and they burst into glowing balls of sparkling light that lit up the sky. All our noisy crackers were echoed by similar lights and noise set off by our immediate neighbours.

By the time we were done with the fireworks, the first blush of the morning was showing in the eastern sky.

Following our fireworks celebrations at home, we walked over to the Chenthitta Devi Temple to offer prayers and get blessings. All along the way people were still blasting fireworks and lighting sparklers.

I grew up very close to Shanthi, my sister who was two years younger than I. We played and shared well, but still fought about silly things. Ammachi would go find a twig to slap our butts, but the joke was that by the time she found the twig, we had resolved our disagreements and were hugging each other, buddies once again.

My second sibling, Jayee, was five years younger than I and all three of us lived in the Chenthitta house until our parents moved to their own home. I loved carrying Jayee around but she was an independent soul. As I remember, she always slid off my hip and wished to walk on her own as soon as she found her *sea-legs.* She did not like the fact that Shanthi and I were best friends and did everything together. Jayee pushed between us to be included in all we did. What she liked best was when I read to her from our old books. Malayalam stories about strong, valiant princes like Lord Rama, or short stories like Jataka tales which had morals at the end. Books were always special in my young life and the biggest treat was when Dad took us all to the biggest English bookstore in town, Higginbothams. I picked up books about Babar the Elephant and Grimm's fairy tales. But Dad wished more for me than the storybooks I loved. He had plans for my learning, more than I ever realized.

First thing in the morning the newspapers arrived in our house. The English ones; *The Times of India* and *The Hindu.* From the day I could string words to make a sentence, Dad made sure I read the English news. Those were the days when we were at the peak of our struggle for Indian independence. My dad wished me to know all the players on both sides. He was a true Gandhian follower. One of my daily assignments was to read the newspaper. When he returned home at night he asked me about what happened in the world. It took me a while but I recognized that he did not ask about the front page news.

He always questioned me about what was on pages 14 to 16 or 15 to 17. Sometimes he asked about sports. World War 2 was over, and all over the world nations were trying to heal and grow back to their original strongholds, or at least mend the rifts between nations.

Dad wished that I grew up knowing all the information about: Gandhiji and Pandit Jawaharlal Nehru in India, and Eisenhower and Churchill and Nasser in the rest of the world making life-altering decisions for our future.

While Dad insisted on all these, Ammachi is the one that put our shoulders to the wheel, so to speak. She is the one who physically sat us down and made us do the reading and the writing and our daily homework for school. Between the two of them I gained knowledge of the workings of the world, which came in handy when I was thrown afloat into another culture and needed to navigate my life and make decisions for our future.

# 11

## The Pilgrimage to Sabarimala and the Ayyappa Temple

**WHEN MY DAUGHTER,** Devi, was only three years old I taught her in earnest to grow up a Hindu as I had from an early age. As a Hindu in the Chicagoland area in 1967, without any family members here for her to observe or follow, all I could do was show her what I practiced as a Hindu.

Unlike me, who grew up immersed in the Hindu traditions and practices all around me, there was not a single Hindu temple in Chicagoland to take her to and show how to kneel prostrate in prayer in front of the statue of a favorite deity. It was not possible to pick flowers from my own garden and carry them to a non-existent temple. I chanted the prayers I had learned to the many deities we believed in, singing them with as much gusto as I could muster. As each year passed, we sang our prayers together, and she learned the words to them with ease. But to me something was missing. It was the power of the chanting and praying I experienced in my youth with my extended family.

In my ammoomma's home, we, the children gathered at dusk to say our prayers. The time when the sun was setting and the moon just started its nocturnal journey across the sky was a special time. It was important for us to say thanks to the day that had passed and to pray for a good outcome for the days yet to come. An oil lamp was lit and we sat in front of it alongside my aunt and Mom and chanted the songs in praise of the different deities. We always started off with one for Lord Ganesha, the god who got rid of obstacles. This was followed by chants for Lord Krishna, Devi Saraswathi, Lekshmi Devi and we ended with an invocation to Devi Parvathi for an auspicious ending, called Mangala Aarati.

I remembered how each month of the year had special significance and different festivals or pilgrimages. Through the years, I tried my best to narrate the stories of each festival to my daughter, the significance of them, and the steps to gaining strength from praying to the different avatars. Unlike me, when I learned every prayer-ritual by watching my family members and by going to the temple, my daughter knew only hear-say to fall back on.

"The fourth month of the year, Vrichigam, arrived, chasing away the rains of the month of Thulam," I told her, "bringing clear skies, cooler air from the mountains, and widespread preparations for the pilgrimage to the *Sabari Mala*, or Sabari Hill, the home of the Temple for Swami Ayyappan."

Just as my father had done when I was a little girl, I recounted the story of Lord Ayyappan who appeared on earth to kill the powerful demoness Mahishi, who terrorized the holy sages as they did their Poojas and meditations in the forests. After his mission on earth was completed, Lord Ayyappan meditated on a hilltop in the mountain range of Western Ghats in our Kerala State in South India. A temple in Lord Ayyappan's name was built here, on a hilltop 1,540 ft. above sea level within the Periyar Tiger Preserve and surrounded by mountains and dense forests.

The pilgrimage to Sabarimala started with a rigorous fast for forty-one days before the actual trip. I learned from my father that ancient Hindu sages believed that periodic fasts or *vrithams* purify the human mind and body. A devotee aspiring for a darshan of Lord Ayyappan has to be pure both mentally and physically and for this, he has to observe a mandatory fast or vritham of forty-one days that usually begins on the first day of the Malayalam month of Vrischikam in mid-November. Like Lord Ayyapan, the renunciant, the devotee is expected to be strictly celibate, eat only vegetarian foods, and is forbidden to drink alcoholic beverages and must immerse himself in prayers, visit temples, and feed the poor.

My dad was a devout Ayyappa follower and took all the rituals and the fasting very seriously in preparation for his annual pilgrimage to Sabarimala.

He told me, my sisters, and my brother, "When you commit yourself to a goal such as serving Lord Ayyappa for the forty-one days of Mandala Pooja, you don't veer from the path chosen for that service. The intense fast, the discipline of the prayers, all set your systems up for the discipline you need in life to achieve all your dreams and goals in education and career." He continued, "At the same time, the prayers you offer to Lord Ayyappan will bring results in your life that are beyond your imagination and beyond belief."

I believed him completely. I did not complain about the vegetarian cuisine for the six weeks or so. In Kerala where many varieties of vegetables grew easily all year long there was no scarcity of choices. My favorites included the gourds and the large green bananas, both of which, cooked with green peas [called moong dhal or red beans] were so delicious I ate them even without the cooked rice served alongside. Garlic, turmeric, and cumin powders were mixed with grated coconut, added to the vegetables, and simmered slow and low until the elements absorbed the flavors. At the very end a garnish with a few curry leaves, [a flavorful leaf from a bush which is from the Neem family] and a teaspoon or two of coconut oil completed the recipe. Not only were these dishes enticing to my taste buds, but I was told over and over again how the turmeric helped to fight infections, and how the garlic and cumin helped digestion. The curry leaves were supposed to protect against worm infestation in the gut, and of course the red pepper, ubiquitous in all South India cooking, not only added flavor, it helped the flow of juices in our stomach to induce digestion as soon as the food entered our stomach.

When Ammachi lectured us on all these benefits, I nodded in agreement while Shanthi rolled her eyes and said how she would rather eat the fish with all the beneficial ingredients added. She could not wait for the end of the forty-one days so she could break the fast.

I was happy to join my father in the daily chanting of prayers. I also prayed that his trip was safe from any tiger attacks or from elephant rampages. I felt close to my father in his dedication and preparation for his pilgrimage. The entire family followed the rules and remained vegetarian, along with my dad [except for the fact that my ammoomma needed fish curry at least once a day]. And of course she got it.

A wood burning fire pit was made with three piles of bricks in the backyard, and the fish was cooked in clay sauce pots used exclusively for cooking fish. Ammoomma ate in the privacy of her own room so that the fish was not served in the dining room. I told Mom it was nice how Ammoomma got her fish without ruining my dad's fast.

At the end of forty days, the preparation for the trip itself was a fascinating process... Each pilgrim wore a two-sided bag on his head. One side held rice grain, moong dhal, red pepper and salt for cooking on the road. On the other side it held rice, a coconut with the surface cleaned and shiny and filled inside with clarified butter. The items on the second side were offerings to give at the temple to propitiate Lord Ayyappan.

On the evening of the fortieth day, our dad and four or five of his co-pilgrims gathered in our front veranda to prepare for the pilgrimage. In those days the forests they travelled through to reach the Sabarimala temple were home to elephants, tigers, and even lions. Living there were snakes of all kinds from *cheras,* rat-snakes (non-venomous but with a nasty bite nevertheless), and deadly cobras and vipers of a few different kinds. They were often disturbed when the humans passed through. Two guides accompanied the pilgrims and carried supplies including gas stoves for cooking. They also carried torches made from bunches of dried coconut fronds, which when lit were flashy and bright enough to wave off tigers once it grew dark.

Thousands of devotees followed the traditional mountainous forest path, approximately twenty-seven miles. Once they had crossed the Pampa River; they climbed a steep mountain called Neelimala and entered into the real temple grounds of Ayyappan. These days people use vehicles to reach the Pampa River by an alternate road. From Pampa, all the pilgrims begin trekking the steep mountain path of Neeli Mala till Sabari Mala. This route is now highly developed with emergency shops and medical aid by the sides. In addition there is supportive aid provided to the pilgrims while climbing the steep slope, which used to be a mere trail through dense jungle. The elderly pilgrims are lifted on bamboo chairs by men and carried to the top.

At the top of the mountain is the temple for *Swami Ayyappan*, Lord Ayyappan. After special pooja services the pilgrims return via the route they trekked up. Each year when my father returned from this pilgrimage, he brought back blessed food. The sweet rice payasam with loads of brown sugar and butter is offered in front of Ayyappa's idol during the pooja, and served to devotees as the blessed food. The ashes from the fire ceremonies were distributed to the family. We wore a mark on our foreheads with a pinch of the white ashes to transfer the power of the pooja that our father conducted to Ayyappa.

The memories of the trips my father took, and the symbolic transfer of blessings to us from the food and offerings, empowered me to do things in life that I normally would be afraid to try. It gave me the confidence to be bold and to never allow fear to stop progress in my projects and my life.

Starting in 1982, I too was practicing/chanting the prayers for the pilgrimage to Sabarimala, even though I did not trek up to the temple atop the mountain. Just following the religious fast and the prayers brought blessings to my life and I saw the fruition of my undertakings. I believe that this particular fast and prayers helped me achieve more in my life than I ever dreamed. Later, I too was able to make the climb up the Sabari Mala and complete the pilgrimage to the Ayyappan temple. When I climbed the eighteen steps to reach the temple I really got a feeling that since I made this difficult pilgrimage, I could do anything I want in life. The newly found confidence in an already self-confident me was awesome.

Throughout the years my daughters have celebrated the special prayer times for Lord Ayyappan. I am certain they too have experienced the power of prayer in their own lives.

1958, The Sivaraam family.
Standing, Shaku, Dad, Jayee, Mom, Hari.
Sitting, Shanthi, Shobha

# 12

## Christmas in Trivandrum

CHRISTMAS HELD AS much importance to my family as any of our Hindu holiday celebrations.

In Trivandrum, you did not need to be a Christian to celebrate the holiday.

Most of the nurses who worked at my ammoomma's hospital were nuns. They lived at the nunnery across the street from the Women and Children's hospital. I remember going to Midnight Mass on Christmas Eve with my ammoomma. All the nuns who were not on duty at the patient wards attended Mass. After Mass, as we walked out, the Mother Superior traditionally would hand Ammoomma a plum cake.

It was really a rum-raisin cake in the traditional Malayalee recipe. The aroma of that dark, luscious cake would linger, imprinting itself on my long-term memory. The rum-soaked raisins felt plump and moist in my mouth as I bit into a piece. The flavor of the special mini-cumin seeds along with a subtle taste of cloves tenderly caressed my palate, and I thought I was in heaven. No other cake, and no other night gave me that feeling.

I believed Christ the Son came to save the world. My family accrued many Christian friends, and we prayed to many avatars of gods on earth, that one more holiday and one more celebration of a Divine being coming to save us was well within my belief spectrum.

Trivandrum's sub-tropic location felt quite tropical in the summer heat, which made it difficult to grow fir or spruce trees. The standard American Christmas tree and the tradition of gift-giving were not part of how we celebrated the holiday. Our Christian friends hung Chinese lanterns by their front porch for the week of Christmas, so we did too. Colorful paper lanterns with bellowed sides were opened up in a cylindrical fashion. They ran about ten to twelve inches in diameter and about fourteen to sixteen inches tall. At the bottom base there was a sturdy cardboard ring. The top rim offered three or four strings so you could suspend the lantern from hooks attached to the ceiling of the front portico. A small candle was wedged into the base of the cardboard. The lantern needed to be hung and balanced very carefully so the flame went straight up. In the dark of the night the rainbow colored paper used to make the lantern project a kaleidoscopic design on the walls and on us. If the wind tilted a lantern too much the paper caught fire and that was the end of the lantern. We were careful not to touch the burning lanterns as they burned out. I never heard of any fire mishaps in our town, unlike Christmas tree fires starting houses on fire.

Shanthi and I attended Catechism classes at Holy Angels' Convent when we entered sixth grade. At the end of the school year there was an overt push with families for students to continue learning the religious classes. While I treasured the biblical stories and the gold tinted *Holy cards* with beautiful scenes of Mother Mary and child, my Hindu background was too ingrained and strong for me to ever entertain converting to Catholicism.

My preference for Hinduism did not make any difference when it came to Christmas celebrations, however.

When my dad decided to enroll me in an English medium school, I ended up in a Catholic convent school. After fourth grade it was an all-girls' school. Holy Angels' Convent was run by nuns and had beautiful, well-kept classrooms, well-kept grounds, large shade trees, and lots of room to roam around at lunch break and while waiting for our rides home. The playground in the center of the facility was covered in sand, was not muddy or weedy, and was surrounded by a variety of flower bushes. The sandy playground was perfect for when we played a modified form of cricket, called 'rounders.' I felt safe here while the statue of our Lady, Mother Mary, watched over us as we played on her playground. Her grotto was a flower garden haven with cooling green ferns to shade her from the sun, making it a serene spot.

Each year at Christmas time our school staged a lavish program for parents, guests, and dignitaries. I was sure to have a spot on stage in one role or the other. For the Nativity scene I acted as one of the three kings, with my curly hair, my gruff voice, and a firm stride that suited the role well. Shanthi was an angel. Due to my characteristics the sisters tended to choose me for the male roles when they taught the class country dancing or polka too, because I picked up the steps quickly and could lead.

Years later, when I visited the Louvre Museum, I made it a point to cover the section where the thirteenth-century Italian paintings were hung. The Holy cards I received at the Holy Angels' Convent showed images of those paintings which made a lasting impression on me. The paintings depicted scenes of the "crib," with Mother Mary, Joseph and the infant Jesus, and scenes of Jesus's life, and the crucifixion. There are some delicate details painted in gold which are unique to the period.

When I was in eighth grade at the Holy Angels Convent School something special happened.

"Shakuntala is not getting on the honor roll this year unless she improves her French pronunciation." Sister Angela was vehement in her opinion as she left our French class and crossed paths with Sister Michaels, who was coming in to teach us algebra for the next hour. I stood there speechless, wondering what Sr. Michaels would say, and if I was even supposed to speak.

"Shakuntala *will* make the honor roll this year," Sister Michaels retorted, defending my honor. "Only yesterday she got 110 out of 100 marks in Algebra, completing extra credits voluntarily." She laughed. "And, you know, dear Sister Angela, Mathematics carries more points toward the 'honor roll' than French does."

Now I had a hard time holding down a chuckle.

Sister Angela was tall, fair, and floated down the corridors as a swan would on smooth waters. At thirteen, we girls admired her beauty queen features, the affected way she turned her whole head to look sideways, the grace with which she waited aside for the rush of students to pass before she proceeded from one class to the next. We aspired to keep our backs straight and walk and talk French like her someday. The words flowed from her mouth like pearls on a satin string, no hesitation, no jarring stops. Sometimes we did not quite comprehend her inflection to indicate dissatisfaction with our lack of fluidity in spoken French, but when we did, we worked harder to practice our pronouns to meet her approval.

Sister Michaels was also tall, but there ended the similarities. She had a dark complexion, a rather big forehead that held a frown most of the time due to the way she worried about everyone, and she rushed through the hallways jostling the girls from one class to the other. And she was loud. For a nun to speak so loud and fast was unusual. She gave us hope that we could make it in this world after all, even if we were not model women like Sister Angela.

I was quite aware that they both liked me. Although I was an above average student, I did not always get on the honor roll. Yet, I was always active in their efforts at fundraisers for the orphanage. I was the first to volunteer to help an injured student or care for any kindergarten student who fell ill in school until the parents came to pick her up. The Tuesday lunch hour found me solving extra-credit math problems on the steps of the chapel with two other classmates. Sr. Micheals warmed up to anyone solving math problems.

I loved to read. When I had to borrow a Charles Dickens book from the library, I had to wait for Sr. Angela to retrieve her huge bunch of keys, and I deliberately chose the one for the cabinet labeled D—E, to find the one I was looking for. No wonder she was in charge of the vast book cabinets lined up against both of the long walls of the assembly hall that acted as the library, when there were no assembly sessions. Those sessions occurred only once every morning for a five-minute prayer session and on special occasions. The way Sr. Angela's long, slender fingers lingered on the book spines before she found the one I wished to read showed how she treasured each book. I think I was special to her because of my love for literature. Fortunately for me, I did make the honor roll that year. I made all of us very happy. I did not realize it then, but as I grew older, Holy Angels' Convent School would make a lasting impression on me. I recognized how privileged I was to be set out into this big, new world with the wealth of knowledge I had acquired from an extensive education and training at the Holy Angels' Convent High School.

During my education from kindergarten to my high school graduation at fifteen, I found this school to be a pleasing place. As I said, after high school, education was followed by two years of what was equivalent to university prep or junior college, and then on to college courses. The sisters did a thorough job of preparing us for college. They also taught us practical skills for life experiences; discipline, problem-solving skills, and intense reading, writing and composition abilities. I learned to knit, crochet, and oil paint. My oil paintings were sold at the school fair to help raise money for the girls' orphanage in the Convent. The sisters loved the fact that I brought them great publicity and how my famous dad, a well-known photographer in town, photographed all of their class photos for free.

My father, my ammoomma and my ammachi were all visionaries who knew our world was changing, that once we were a free nation I would be the beneficiary of opportunities not afforded to them in their youth.

Even in my generation most of my family and friends did not attend private schools, and very few went to all-English-Medium schools.

The following poem, which I would write as an adult looking back at this time, captures memories of those convent-school days.

## *Verbenas*

Verbenas remind me of how

for a freshman class project in high school,

we started a garden under my farming guidance


one half the plot had flowers; the other, vegetables

'twas in nineteen fifty-three

in the hot and muggy Trivandrum town


on barren red clay, with help from mounds of cow manure, we
planted verbenas

beside the beans, eggplant and green peas


no tilling to do 'cause

Ramu and John were our gardening help.

we just had to plant and water the many precious seedlings


'*Verbenas,*' I suggested, and the entire class did agree

Oh! the colors, the leaves, and especially the aroma!

of course, we needed a fence to keep hungry bunnies at bay


in the three years following,

the high school garden project blossomed

each class had their own plot, and competitions were held

every year my class won the trophy

I was master gardener at thirteen thanks to the

strong gardening genes from my mother and aunt before me


alas! now when I plant verbenas,

even fences can't keep the rabbits away

I till, toil, plant and water, and my verbenas turn into

a tasty lunch for the bunnies around. Still, I will keep on planting
verbenas

not only for their subtle scents

shades of vibrant-violet, rosy-red and brilliant-blues...


but also for the high school memories

where resonance of girlfriends' laughter uplift my spirit,

light a glow on my cheek and place a smile on my face


Shaku Rajagopal

*Verbenas in my garden*

# 13

## A Wedding Celebration

SARADAMMA, MY AMMACHI, walked gracefully and slow toward the floral gazebo where her bridegroom was already seated, awaiting their nuptials. Ammachi's face glowed and to me she looked royal and beautiful in a sandalwood colored, pure silk saree, touting a red border with star-shaped floral designs in golden thread scattered through its entire six yards. She wore a twenty-two carat gold necklace that she designed especially for the occasion. It hung down about an inch below her collarbone, and rested an inch above the neckline of her gold-colored choli blouse. She also wore a long two-layered gold chain with gold leaves in the shape of beaten rice which linked to small gold balls. This added just enough shine and glitz to make her sparkle, but not too much and not gaudy. She was one of the classiest ladies I knew, and she was the favorite person in my nine-year-old world.

My ammachi was a research chemist in Organic Chemistry at the Travancore University in Thiruvananthapuram. She was a smart, charismatic, industrious lady who took care of Ammoomma's business affairs, catered to her physical comforts, and with efficiency maintained Ammoomma's complicated household.

In 1939 Ammachi received admission for medicine at the Lahore University in North India. However, World War II had broken out and the Indian leaders put a halt to our fight for independence from the

British and joined the British army in the fight against the European and Japanese army. At that point Ammoomma decided it would be too risky to send Ammachi away to school far from home and instead Ammachi joined the research program in the university. Her research concentrated on alkaloids. They had their own research laboratory in their own building and a separate administration to manage their affairs. This gave her a lot of freedom to conduct her research. Having other students study under her guidance proved she was a well-respected teacher.

Ammoomma placed importance on education and career and did not hesitate to postpone any wedding plans for her oldest daughter, Saradamma. My mother, Retnamma, was three years younger and had no wish to go to college; she married at the age of sixteen and started a family long before Ammachi.

Ammachi's wedding was fixed. Her future bridegroom, named Ramakrishna Pillai, worked in the City Corporation offices. Their marriage was arranged by Ammoomma and his oldest sister, and according to the reading by the astrologer who studied their horoscopes, the wedding was to take place at the auspicious time of 2:30 a.m. In our communities weddings were conducted in the yards of our homes or in the temple courtyards. Because Ammoomma's house was in the middle of town and had a small backyard, it was decided the wedding would take place in the backyard of my mother's house.

Before Ammachi's wedding, a floral landscaped yard with brilliant colors surrounded my mother's home. A six foot tall cement wall delineated the front yard from the back where the pink roses, deep red roses, and yellow roses with the orange borders, all intermingled in a heavenly scent. The low, cement parapet walls in the front yard were beautified with a border of roses and low-lying purple daisies barely eight inches tall that hugged close to the base of the tall tea roses. The backyard included tall tamarind trees, two large fruit-bearing mango trees and clumps of banana palms close to a watering well. All the plants were watered from the well. In addition, my mother had white, sweet-smelling jasmines climbing on the walls and onto the bark of trees, strengthened by thin coir-strings tied to the lower branches. When I walked around her yard, the roses and jasmines mingled sweet layers of heady perfume throughout the air which made me feel giddy. Once you were there, you never forgot that feeling. In addition my mother grew passion vines on trellises leaning against the cement walls. In summer she picked the passion fruit before the birds discovered them and she ripened them in straw beds in the back veranda. She dropped their fleshy insides into our lemonade, and with the dark seeds covered with fluffy white flesh they looked like floating eyes in our lemonade.

There were bee-hives she had just started. They too had to be displaced. But moved to the area where the tamarind trees stood, they did not do well. I don't remember seeing them in her yard later in life.

When the yard was cleared for the wedding, Amma lost many of her garden plants. She had no qualms as she pulled them off with a smile for the true happiness of seeing her sister get married. We had all waited a long time for this event.

The night of the wedding all the relatives brought presents for her, silver bowls and a silver sprayer for rose water, cooking pots, and coffee-makers. Ivory figurines of Ganesha and different deities were from Ammomma's colleagues and even from her patients. Close relatives brought gold ornaments, chains, and gold bangles.

The most fun was how many of the guests brought toys, books, blouses and skirts as gifts for Shanthi and me. Being that we were Ammoomma's immediate granddaughters, many guests, especially those from out of town, showered us with favors. We made off like bandits from all the loot we gained. The best part was we got to stay up as long as we wanted, which was all through the night, of course.

The bridegroom's party, including his oldest sister, two younger brothers whom I had met before, and four other siblings and families arrived about half an hour before the auspicious moment set for the wedding. This was the beginning of the wedding festivities. Their party was met and welcomed by my mother and my uncle. Shanthi and I and seven of our cousins walked in a procession carrying brass trays of flowers with small oil lamps in which little wicks were lit and glowing. Older cousins and our aunts accompanied us to make sure the lit lamps were held safely. When we reached the bridegroom's party, my uncle handed a bouquet of flowers to the bridegroom, and placed a garland of flowers on his neck in welcome for the occasion. My mother blessed him with a mark of sandalwood paste from the temple on his forehead. The whole procession of girls and family members led him to the floral gazebo. In the middle of the gazebo a plank of wood covered with while muslin cloth was ready for him to be seated. Here he waited for his bride. To his left a tall oil lamp carrying many wicks was lit and glowing, beside an array of a barrel of rice grain with a bunch of flowers from a coconut palm stuck in the middle representing abundance. In addition a large tray of flowers and fruits, including bananas and oranges, was also placed in front of the lamp to propitiate the gods.

Now it was the bride's turn to be led ceremoniously to this podium. From the main house she followed our welcome band toward the bridegroom. The light from the lamps shed a soft glow on her face. She smiled at us tenderly as she walked up the step to the podium. She turned around and with both palms opposed in a prayer fashion bowed down toward the family and friends gathered to obtain their blessing. I glanced at Ammoomma seated in the front row and saw her raise her right palm in a sign of blessing to her oldest daughter. Ammachi was directed by her uncle to take her seat on the left side of the groom. Amidst loud live music, drums blasting, and saxophones and flutes playing Ammachi placed a rose garland on the groom's neck accepting him as her husband. He reciprocated and placed a garland on her neck. He was now officially and forever our 'Valiachan.' it literally meant *Big Father*. For us it meant *father's older brother*.

Up until then the two persons who enjoyed Ammachi's freedom were Shanthi and I. Ammachi had four other friends and colleagues who took us to the museum, the zoo, the Sri Chitra Art Gallery, and the Town Library on a regular basis. I knew all that would change once she became married, but what I found out was that it only got better.

Instead of losing her because of marriage, we gained one more person to love in Valiachan. When Valiachan came into our family, he accepted the fact that Ammachi had raised Shanthi and me as her own daughters. When the newlyweds were invited to the homes of friends and family for welcome dinners, they took us along. We also gained a whole extended family through him. His sisters became our *Appachis,* or *father's sisters* and their children became our 'cousins.' Ammachi had a loving and inclusive attitude to friends and family, and the two of us gained a lot of love from our new extended family Ammachi married into.

1945  Ammachi, Shaku, Shanthi

1949  Valiachan, Ammachi

# 14

## Vishu and Vishu-Kani, Vishu Celebration

THE AIR IS hot. It is very, very hot. Midsummer. The schools are on summer vacation, and the *Konna maram,* or Cassia fistula trees are loaded with bunches of yellow *Konna poovu,* Konna flowers. In my opinion, no other flowers except the sunflowers reflect the sun's energy on us like the Konna flowers.

Trying to look at the yellow flowers will make you squint. They are so bright. That is the picture that comes to mind when I think of April in Kerala.

This was a very special month for us kids because we received silver coins as gifts from Ammoomma, Dad, Mom, Ammachi and our uncles. All we had to do was smile. And, this is the month we celebrate the divinity within us.

The Malayalam word "kani" literally means "that which is seen first," so "Vishukkani" means "that which is seen first on Vishu." The Vishukkani consists of a ritual arrangement of auspicious articles intended to signify prosperity. On the night previous to the Vishu celebration, my mom and Ammachi set up an altar with a mirror in the center, and auspicious articles arranged in front of it: coconut, fresh vegetables, fruits, flowers, mainly the yellow bunches of Kanikkonna, and coins. Long gold chains and necklaces are hung on the mirror. These are arranged in a bell metal vessel called *uruli* in the pooja room of the house. A lighted bell metal oil lamp called *nilavilakku* is also placed alongside. The oil lamp is lit to cast an aura of blessing upon the whole lot. This is arranged the night before Vishu.

At the crack of dawn of the day of Vishu, my mother led me and Shanti to the prayer room of the house, with our eyes closed and covered with her hands. This is so the first sight of the new season would be the altar with the Vishukkani. It is the age-old belief of Malayalees that an auspicious *kani* at dawn on the Vishu day will bring good luck for the entire year. As a result, the *Vishukkani* is prepared with immeasurable care to make it a positive sight and bring a wonderful, prosperous year.

At the moment of the Vishukani, I saw my reflection in the mirror placed in the pooja room. My reflection was wearing the gold chain and necklace hung on the mirror. I was taught that on this day we pray to the divinity within ourselves as the first act of the morning. All put together, the ambiance makes you feel like you are the deity you are praying to.

Even today, when I think of the Vishu Kani I get the special feeling of praying to my inner powers.

We chanted special prayers to Lord Krishna, describing his lotus-petal-shaped eyes, describing the naughty escapades, and praying for his blessing.

The best was yet to come. Ammoomma sat on the drawing room couch jingling silver coins in her palm. We lined up in front of her with open palms and she place a coin in each right palm. Our eyes lit up, and we barely took time to bow before her to say thank you. Then we ran off to find Dad, Mom, Ammachi, and our uncles, to get our Vishu-kaineettam from each of them.

After baths and breakfast we waited to see the farm workers visit to receive the Vishukaineetam from Ammoomma. They feasted with a Sadya for lunch.

In the evening we walked to the temple and often many of our relatives came to visit and stayed for dinner. Invariably we were given more coins from them also as vishukaineettam.

One year my ammoomma bought a car just a few days before Vishu. This was a historic event in my life.

*I know of a character in a short story I read when I was young, who stopped all arguments by standing tall in his full height of 5' 6", and declaring--*

**"entuppuparku oru ana ondarrnu." "my grandfather owned an elephant."**

*That effectively quieted the crowd every time.*

*His story trumped all others that day.*

I wish to declare like he did in his story--

**"my ammoomma owned a Morris Minor car."**

I was ten years old when my doctor Ammoomma decided to buy a car.

My ammoomma provided us with all physical comforts we needed and more. A beautiful home, exquisite silks to wear, and jewels galore; we needed nothing. But, then, there were certain things in life that she did not deem necessary.

My father, her son-in-law, would tell her repeatedly, "you need to buy a car. It is time that you went to the hospital and to your temple visits in a decent car of your own."

"No, no!" she protested. "The hospital is close enough to walk to. To the temple I can always take a cab; for any other trips Annachi (a patient who had a car), will send me his car anytime I ask. That is all we need." She was quite vehement about that.

I remember going to kindergarten at the Holy Angel's Convent in a bullock cart. At five years of age, riding in the morning in a bullock cart was an adventure. The floor of the bullock cart, which was mainly used to transport grain and vegetables to the market, was lined by a layer of hay to make it less hard for my two older cousins and me. A jute bag was spread over the hay in a futile attempt to screen out the dust from dirtying our clothes. The bumpy ride over graveled roads ruined by heavy rains, and the noisy horns of the few cars on the road at the time did not bother me much because I was busy looking at the nodding heads of the bullocks, and the multi-colored ropes, and tinkling bells tied to their bulky necks.

But such entertainment did not last long.

At the end of the first week, my ammoomma decided it was not proper for her *ponnumol* to arrive at school smelling of hay. Even worse, I was told later, she could hardly wait to give me a bath once I returned home from school. Now that I think of it, I am sure that ammoomma decided it was not worth the extra soap and water expended to remove the smell of hay out of my thick curly hair every evening. She was frugal, but pragmatic. And, thus, the bullock cart rides only lasted one week.

From then on we started riding a horse and buggy to school and back. That, I really liked! Seated high, I could see a lot more of the road and the world. The swaying of the carriage to the rhythm of the clickety-clack of the horses was exciting. The inside of the carriage even had a regular cotton floral lining. And the wooden seats had leather cushions, albeit thin ones.

Two years later, when I was in 2nd grade, my cousins, both girls much older than I, transferred to a different school. My kochanujathi, my little sister, started school, and that is when the horse and buggy were dismissed and we started taking the convent-school-bus for our daily transport.

Three years later, one more sister of mine joined us at Holy Angel's Convent School. The bills for the convent-bus were adding up. Three of us needed bus rides. Also, my aunt, a lecturer at the university, was taking a cab every day. My ammoomma decided it was healthier for her pocketbook if we had our own car. There were lengthy discussions of buying a used car, one of those huge old Ford cars with the wing tips at the rear. Why they decided on a Morris Minor, I do not remember. I do remember the only color choices were black or white. The decision was unanimous. Black it was.

My ammoomma even took this *ponnumol* on her trip to Maraikar motors to order the car. Then came the wait! I don't remember how long, but it seemed like eternity to a ten-year-old.

Now started the process of finding a 'driver' for the car. No one in the family could drive a car. None was expected to. Many qualified drivers were interviewed, and I asked my mom why it was so complicated. "All he needs to know is to drive a car, right? So why all this fuss?"

"To take you precious ones all over the place we need someone that is more than *just able to drive*," my mom informed me. "We have to have a family man, and one that we can trust."

Thus it was 'Krishna Pillai Chettan,' our driver, who came to be an important member of our household even before the car arrived.

The day came when the car was ready to be picked up. Dressed up in our finery, my sister and I accompanied my ammoomma to go get the car. A shiny black Morris Minor! What a delightful sight! Our very own car. And the new leather smell was delightful. We were enchanted. Our first trip was to the Ganesha Temple. Lord Ganesha is the God who has an elephant head, and when we pray to him he gets rid of obstacles, ensuring success in any of our endeavors. Seven coconuts were cracked in front of Lord Ganesha to propitiate the Lord. We received the *prasadam* or blessed offerings from the temple, which included flowers, bananas and sandalwood paste used for the prayer services. The new car received a *chandana-kuri,* a mark on her front panel with the blessed sandalwood paste. We stopped to offer flowers at the Chenthitta Devi Kshetram and returned home. The entire trip had the feel of having been to the *Aarattu* procession or a *Pooram,* two different festivals in town we enjoyed going to. Even better, we felt that Vishu had come early with a larger gift than our usual monetary gifts of Vishu.

Years later, as a young struggling resident physician in this country, there were many occasions when I could not buy the things I wanted, and many plans were thwarted, or dreams postponed due to lack of funds or lack of time. At those times I would say to myself, "My ammoomma had a Morris Minor; I too can make wishes come true. Even if we have to wait a while, all our dreams can come true." Yes, that is still true.

And, yes, I do proudly proclaim: *"my doctor ammoomma did have a Morris Minor car."*

# 15

## Rains of Idavapathi

IT RAINED AND rained and rained.

The loud thunder and flash of lightning gave a ghostly feel to the already dark place because of the low-lying clouds of the monsoons.

Our summer vacation kept us children home from school mid-April to mid-June. The first six weeks of that vacation were spent indoors, however, because it was too hot to do anything outside until close to sundown. Now we were into the third month of the vacation. The name of the month in Malayalam was **Idavam**. It is the month that starts in the second week of the Gregorian month of June and goes through the middle of July.

My town, Thiruananthapuram in South India, lay bathed by the waters of the Arabian Sea on the west. Just seven miles east was well protected by the Sahya Mountains, which were part of the Arabian Ghats. The mountains were covered by lush dark green forests of ebony and teakwood, acres and acres of rubber plantations, and forests of cultivated clove trees, cinnamons, and cardamom plants.

As you descend the mountains toward the wild waves of the Arabian Sea, you cut through green paddy fields of rice that look like huge soft green carpets as far as the eye can behold. Rice was our staple. Footpaths separating square acres of the rice fields appear like border designs woven on the surface of the silken carpets. In my mind there is no other place on earth where you can see such emerald green fields as in this corner of the Earth. We have even named our State of Kerala "God's own Country."

And then there are farms that occupy lower-lying areas where banana palms are grown, with square-shaped tilled ground about six feet square around each banana palm. Around the banana palms, under the shade of their wide and long banana leaves, the red spinach grew strong and formed ruby red patches until they were harvested before they went to seed. A few patches would be let go to seed, the seeds collected before the heavy rains.

The rice fields extended down close to the beaches and there the coconut palms took over. The bracken water of the slightly salty and clear rainwater mix was optimal for the coconuts to grow. In this area the strong ammonia smell of the cow manure, which was the main food for the coconut palms, would be offensive unless your nose grew immune to it, which was the case for us who grew up around them.

If you were willing to put your muscle to good use, and willing to farm the rich soil, there was never a need to starve in this land called Kerala, the land of the coconuts. Apart from the coconut giving great flavor to the fish, tapioca, and the rice dishes, the white meat inside the coconut shell is dried and oil extracted. The coconut oil is used for cooking, lighting the lamps and treating the girls' hair so it grew long and strong.

The husk of the coconut was soaked and beaten, and the fibers pulled to braid into ropes called *coir*. The coir mats made from thinner rope strands were world famous. I remember being told that Mercedes Benz Company had an exclusive contract with the companies in Kerala, in a town called Aleppey, about two and a half hours from my hometown. Parts of the coconut tree, including the tall, long log-like single stem, were used to make rafts which carried the coir ropes, the coconut oil, rice and other grains, black pepper, cardamom, cloves and even nutmeg products to the ports where ships awaited. Years ago, black pepper sent to European countries brought so much wealth to the land of Kerala, that it was called "black gold."

In my ammoomma's home, we had fish for lunch and dinner since the fishermen brought fish to the market in the morning and evening. We had an errand boy who went to the market twice a day.

The smell of fish never bothered me, but it bothered my dad, who was a vegetarian. My ammoomma, on the other hand, could not eat a meal without fish curry. I loved the flavor of the fish curry with coriander, cumin, ginger, and hot red pepper powder added to it. While it simmered slowly over the wood-burning fire, a sour sauce from the dried fruit of the tamarind tree was added till the fish was well cooked. This fish curry over warm steaming cooked rice still beats any gourmet dish I can imagine. And this is coming from someone who loves a good steak with baked potato on the side.

The monsoons come around the last part of May and beginning of June. The rains are a welcome relief from the summer heat and are needed for the rice fields as well as the vegetable farms. But by middle of June, when the raging winds knock down coconut palms and trample the vegetables, everyone starts complaining. We are used to rain—and lots of it. But too much of it also threatens the crops, which is unacceptable. And yet, what can you do?

As children, however, we didn't care.

Just before the monsoons started, we always went school-shopping. New clothes, new umbrellas, new schoolbags, and new lunch containers. The lunch was usually rice mixed with curds, what we call yogurt, a vegetable dish, beans, or spinach or moong dhal, which is split small green peas special to South India. A spoonful of pickle will be set to one side of the steel lunch box, which is not a box at all. It is a two-tiered cylindrical canister with a tight lid. After lunch, we'd drink water at the tap outside the lunchroom. If the water splashed on our clothes, it was not a big deal because in the heat of the noon sun the skirt would dry by the time we walked back to our classroom.

Schools re-opened after the summer break, smack in the middle of the monsoons, but it was better to sit in classrooms cooled by the rains and wind rather than boiling in sweltering summer sun.

One of the things I missed most after moving to the Chicago

area was the monsoon rains. When it grew dark and cloudy, and the thunder raged outside, our older cousins closed the windows and we huddled as we told ghost stories. Although the room was dark, the lightning flashed into the room through the transoms atop the windows and startled us at the spookiest moments of the story.

One such story was about a beautiful maiden appearing to a man alone by the road where his bike was stranded. She offers to take him to safety from the rain. She has long dark curly hair that came down past her waist. In an all-white saree and blouse outfit, she appears eerily beautiful. Once she starts speaking, he is mesmerized and cannot say no.

So he walks with her deep into a forest. She stops on the forest-path and he sees that her back is hollow, that he can see her insides when her hair moves. He recognizes her as a *"yakshi,"* A supernatural beauty who lures men into the forest. He screams as she transforms into a witch-like form and goes for his jugular with her fangs.

It always happened that the thunder and lightning would increase at this juncture of the story. The younger ones screamed and cried. The older ones shushed them so we could listen to the rest of the story. So my cousin would finish telling it. Just before the man passes out, the yakshi tells him it is her revenge for his great-grandfather killing her unjustly many years ago. And with that, the man blacks out.

The next morning they find his dead body inside the forest not too far from his disabled bike. Fang marks on his neck and a long lock of black curly hair left on his still chest are the only clues of what happened to him.

We would cling to each other, the younger ones crying, until the storms passed.

On the days the rains were just rains and no thunderstorms were present, we were allowed to go out and play catch in the rain.

In the States, on warm summer days when it rained I went out with my children and their cousins and played catch and did cartwheels on the lawn. Just thinking of those times keeps me young at heart.

Years later I still played in the rain with my grandchildren, but did not try to do cartwheels.

*1951, from L to R, Hari, Shanthi, Shaku and Jayee.*
*On a rainy day our Dad gathered us in his studio*
*for a siblings' portrait.*

# 16

## An Addition to the Chenthitta Family

**STARTING MY FIRST** year of high school at thirteen years of age provided a level of maturity, but it wasn't until Ammachi called me and Shanti into the drawing room that I knew I was about to earn more responsibilities. Ammachi sounded deep in thought, "My cousin, Indira (daughter of Doctor Ammoomma's oldest sister), is coming to live with us." We knew her well. She was Indira Kunjamma to us, Kunjamma means little mother, which is what we called mother's younger sisters, and female cousins younger than my mother

"Indira has rheumatic fever and it has affected her heart. She will be on bed rest for a while and will need more care than her mother or siblings can give. So we are going to take care of her."

"Rheumatic fever? Will Usha catch it from her?" I was worried for my three-year-old cousin, Ammachi's daughter.

"No, Indira had strep throat a few weeks ago and that affected her heart. Then she developed a murmur in her heart and became very sick. She won't give the infection to anyone now." Ammachi's voice was soothing and reassuring. I trusted her completely. Shanthi and I helped Ammachi prepare the additional bedroom with clean sheets and pillows. She explained, "Indira needs complete bed rest with the exception of walking over to the toilet, for which she will need support along the way. We also need to help Kamalakshi in the kitchen to help feed Indira, and help give Indira sponge baths."

Later that morning Indira Kunjamma's brother brought her to Chenthitta house and we settled her in her bedroom. I felt very responsible and also wanted to know more about her condition. Later that day when Ammoomma returned from the hospital I went to her room and asked her questions. "Why did Indira Kunjamma get the rheumatic fever? What exactly happened to her heart? What is a murmur?" I was curious.

"Come, sit down." Ammoomma patted her bed. I sat down. "We don't know why some people get damage to the heart following a strep throat. Actually the damage is to the heart valves, mainly the mitral valve. When the blood goes through damaged heart valves they make a specific noise we call a heart murmur." She continued. "It happened to Indira and we will make sure she receives bed rest and more penicillin, and we will order a specialist to come see her while she is here."

This was my first participation with direct patient care before I went to medical college to become a doctor. Ammachi and family teamed together to nurse Indira back to health. While she recuperated, I helped home school her through some of the high school curriculum she had to drop out of. After six months she was allowed to return to school. She was admitted to Holy Angels Convent school, in the Malayalam division, which offered the same curriculum as the government schools. We finished high school the same year, even though she was almost two years older than me and one year ahead of me in school before her heart problems.

I saw how committed Ammachi and Ammoomma were in their care for Indira Kunjamma, and how their love made miracles happen. Indira continued to live with us, finished school, and became a nursery school teacher. Now she had a chance of having a career of her own. In those days patients with mitral stenosis were advised to avoid marriage and childbirth due to a lack of guidelines for maternal care during childbirth, and too many mortalities. However, Indira defied the limited guidelines and did get married later and lived a very fulfilled life. She did not bear children of her own. She mentored and watched over two nephews during her lifetime, and stayed close to them until she passed away at the ripe old age of seventy-nine.

I consider it a great blessing to be part of a family that took her under their wing and accepted her as part of our immediate family. Acceptance was the norm with my family. When a friend or relative needed help, we did not shy away from their illness, or shut out those in need of a place to live while completing their college degree. Our family gladly fed and cared for them during their stay.

# 17

# Karkadakam, the Ramayana Month

**KARKADAKAM, (THE LAST** Malayalam month of the year,) falls from the middle of July to the middle of August, and at the end of the month the New Year comes, bearing brown sheaves of rice waving high in the fields ready for harvest. Being a year-end, everybody prepares to get rid of the old, (old clothes, old pillows, old furniture, and old pots and pans) do a thorough in-and-out cleaning of their houses, and prepare the land for the New Year.

In my home the floors in the house were polished cement, and in the drawing room it was dark grey colored cement. Even when we were young girls, Shanthi and I took part in this cleaning process. We both were excited to pour buckets of water onto the polished cement floors in our house. We used brooms to scrub the floor and swept the water out on to the verandah and then into the yard. We had fun sweeping out the water and often splashed each other. As long as we did not make a mess on the walls and no one slipped on the wet floor and got hurt, we did not get into trouble. If any one of us misbehaved or became unruly, we were ousted from this fun job.

The one thing we learned early in life was if we hurt ourselves we got spanked on our butt. It was as if we did it on purpose, but of course we didn't. If I fell down the stairs Ammachi was right there with one *hot potato* (that is what I called it when I got spanked on my butt), for being careless. If we were stoic enough not to cry when we fell, we definitely started sobbing and the tears flowed when we got spanked for it. It took many years before we realized we did not get spanked for the fall; it was Ammachi's way of expressing her frustration at not being able to protect us and a warning to make us more careful.

The rice fields turned gold and were ready to be harvested at this time. The sheaves are taken to Ammoomma's property in Kaudiar, an adjacent town a half hour from where we lived. My mom and Ammachi took the bus to Ammoomma's rice fields to supervise. At the time Ammoomma's sister and family lived on that property. The ground was beaten flat, watered down and dried, making it ready for the beating of the rice sheaves to free the grain. The rice grain with the husk still on is called *nellu.* This is spread out in the sun, and once dried, the rice was poured into huge chute bags of nellu and carried away to be processed. Once dried and processed the rice was then brought to our home to store in wooden compartments in a room attached to our kitchen. There were two compartments or *ara* in this built-in storage--one for the nellu rice with husk on, and the other one for the unhusked clean rice ready for cooking. Every few months the husked rice was taken to be unhusked for us to cook.

The field hands, the ladies cleaning the rice, and the people carrying the rice back and forth, were all paid in bushels or half bushels of the rice in various stages. Later on, when my parents moved out to the suburb of Kaudiar, the processing took place in my mom's front yard and my sister, Shanthi, supervised the whole process.

It has to be the farmer's gene I inherited from my great grandfather that fascinated me about this process of our staple food. When I went back to visit and saw the rice harvesting, the farmer in me longed to return to that simple life and all activities close to the Mother Earth.

But I am not one to break down and cry. I would return to my home in Palatine, a suburb of Chicago, and immerse myself with gusto in the modern life I opted for. Yet I took all opportunities to grow a variety of vegetables and many kinds of flowers, especially roses in my garden, despite pushing myself to make time. I have come to realize my opportunities were there to make up for the things I had to leave behind. I fully appreciated what I built/grew here without wasting my time pining for what I did not have.

This being the last month of our Dravidian calendar, a special prayer offering called *Bali pooja* also called *Shraddha, or Pithru pooja*, was done which included rites and rituals to honor the souls of our ancestors who had passed away from this earth. The ritual is called *Karkadaka Bali.* Karkadakam was the name of the month and Bali the ritual of inviting the ancestors to come receive our prayer offerings. I did not do the Bali pooja when I lived in Thiruananthapuram. I saw my uncle perform the ritual. He cooked white rice mixed with sesame seeds which is the main item used for this pooja, plus basil leaves, flowers, red kumkum powder, sandalwood paste, and water for purification. Sitting Hindu style, cross-legged on the ground, he followed the instructions of the *poojari*, priest, in charge. First, he rolled the cooked rice into three balls and placed them on a banana leaf. The ritual started with his chanting mantras to invoke the spirits of my grandfather, his father, as well as his ancestors to descend from their heavenly abode to receive his special prayers and rituals to honor them. Next, flowers and incense were offered as the priest continued chanting more mantras that my uncle repeated after the poojari. After a while the poojari said the spirits had accepted the offerings. The rice balls, the flowers, and the remaining pooja items were placed on to the grass in the back of the house. My uncle then clapped toward the sky and waited. A few minutes later, black ravens flew out of nowhere and pecked and ate the rice with sesame seeds. We, the children, were told the black ravens represented the ancestors. If other birds came but the ravens did not, it meant that one or more of the ancestors were not pleased with the offerings or the attitude of the person performing the honoring rituals. At that point the family would consult an astrologer to check what remedial prayers needed to be done to make the ancestral spirits happy. I was told that the additional poojas were directed toward propitiating a particular deity, or sometimes a planet such as *Sani,* Saturn. Whatever ritual or pooja the astrologer advised, we took it very seriously in order to counter any ill effects that were being directed toward the family.

This is also the Ramayana month. We read the story of Lord Rama and how he removed the cruel ten-headed demon, King Ravana, from earth, after Ravana had abducted Rama's wife, Sita, and took her to Sri Lanka where he was king. The story of Rama was a treatise in the role we play in our life on earth. Lord Vishnu made his avatar on this Earth as Rama, the crown prince of Ayodhya, and he was the poster-child/man for the way he conducted himself, fulfilling his duties to his father at the cost of his crown and his wife. Chanting the verses of *Ramayanam,* the story of Rama, was not easy for us children and we needed help from friends who specialized in the proper pronunciation and the intonations for the chanting.

For many years an elder relative visited our house to chant the *Ramayanam* and talk about the life of Rama; we sat enraptured as we listened. It was the discipline, the morals learned, and the chanting Rama's name with total dedication that brings special blessings to us without fail. All through my life, the practice of total immersion in prayers and surrender to God's will has helped me stay sane and content when unforeseen things happen.

As my children grew, I taught them about how dedicated Rama was to his father's needs and how he followed his belief of Dharma, at a great cost of worldly comforts for him as well as his wife, Sita. The morality stories of Rama's life were impressed upon my girls the best I could.

Raj and I did follow the path of our Dharma in leaving our comforts of family and coming over here to promote our education as well as provide a better life for the little ones back home.

The day after I came to the States I needed to buy rice, my staple food item, so I went to the store called National. I was amazed at the variety of goods all displayed for purchase in one store. I learned it was called the supermarket. Unlike the stores back home where the vegetables were at the *Vegetable store*, or the rice, grains, spices, etc. were found at the *Provisions store,* all food items were in this "National" store. I was excited to see how clean and how organized the items were in the aisles. I could have spent the whole evening roaming them except that I had to return home to cook dinner.

It took me a while to locate the rice; I tried looking for wooden bins with no success. Then by chance, I found bags of rice stacked in rows on the shelves. I saw at least three different kinds, white long grain, white par-boiled, brown, etc. I saw that the par-boiled was much more expensive, so I purchased the long grain kind. It tasted okay, but later when I tasted the parboiled kind, I could not wait to be able to buy the more expensive par boiled rice as soon as we could afford it. The other feature that amazed me was the size of the packages: 2lb package, 5lb. package and on up to 20 lb. packages. I needed more than the smaller packages of rice on a regular basis, but I had to pick a lighter package I could carry, even though it was only two blocks away to my apartment. Having come from a place where rice was my staple food, most of my dishes have rice as a main ingredient or as a side dish. Even our breakfast foods were Idli or steamed rice-cakes, Dosa or thin crepe-like pancakes made up of ground rice and urad (a black pea) which was cleaned and the lentil ground up for the batter. Even our salty and sweet snacks had rice flour for their base.

I had expected lifestyle changes when I left home, but when I returned seven and a half years later to visit, I was shocked to see the extent of the changes and the affect it made on our daily life even with the simplest things such as rice. Since the 1940s things have changed. More people travelling to and from North India are adapting to the food items such as chappathi, barota etc. made of wheat and wheat flour. Thus, they had replaced rice-based food items in our menu in the South and vice versa, more rice dishes such as idli have become favorites in the North. This was totally different from when I was growing up in Thiruvananthapuram. I am still amazed at how a hot dish of cooked rice with some yogurt and a spoonful of spicy, diced, lime pickle has remained my comfort food even now, fifty-some years after I left my birthplace and have come to love and embrace this adopted land as my own. It could have to do with the love and caring I felt from the people who fed me as a child, or the safe place where I got to know it in my early life. The magic of food and the love of food is inexplicable.

# 18

## A New Year and New Beginnings

**OUR DRAVIDIAN CALENDAR** in Kerala had the New Year starting in the middle of August on the Gregorian calendar. The first month, Chingam, ended in the middle of September. We were not confused with the overlaps. While the official calendars for business, taxes, and all legal transactions followed the Gregorian calendar, we celebrated our birthdays according to our special calendar. To make life even more complex, and interesting, our actual birthdays were celebrated according to our birth star.

The month of Chingam brought in the harvests and celebrations galore. *Krishna Jayanthi,* the day of Lord Krishna was born, and *Ganesha Chathurthi*, the birthday of Lord Ganesha the elephant-headed deity were the most colorful ones. The Ganesha chathurthi festival includes the making of small clay idols, placed in the homes and after a week of prayers these are carried in processions to the sea or a large body of water such as a lake while singing hymns and chanting Vedic prayers, the idols are floated into the water. In Kerala, the celebration of Onam festival outshines and surpasses all other festivals in this month.

A very significant political element launched these processions in the 1800s. Before that, the events were more home-based and community-based. However, in 1892, the British government made a proclamation that banned gatherings of over twenty people, even for religious reasons. It was interesting, yet disturbing, that the Muslim community and their prayer sessions were excluded from this rule. Apparently the Muslim leaders put pressure on the British rulers at the time to get this exclusion. This invoked protests in the Hindu communities. Sri. Lokamanya Tilak, an Indian freedom fighter and social reformer, led large processions carrying the clay idols of Ganesha and revived the public celebration of Ganesha Chathurthi.

There was one radio in our house. Everybody gathered around it to listen to music programs, news, and radio-dramas. On Saturday mornings a character named *'Radio-ammavan,'* meaning radio-uncle held a program for children with children performing skits, singing songs, and telling stories. Periodically, singing competitions were held for all age groups of children from five years old to sixteen years. There were also competitions in chanting *bhajans* and prayers.

Ammachi's husband, our *Valiachan,* meaning big father, or senior father, was an avid cricket fan. When a cricket game was being broadcast, he had the rank to monopolize the radio. This went on for hours, and we were not able to listen to our programs at that time.

It was on that radio that I heard the news about our great leader, Mohandas Karamchand Ghandi. A very long-standing occupation of India by the British had affected our culture and social systems. My Dad and Ammachi taught us of the effects of the British rule and how the Congress party and other groups of freedom fighters were rising up against the British rule.

As soon as I could read, my father, an ardent Gandhian follower, had me follow the Indian Independence movement in the newspapers, on the radio, and the Sunday matinée at the movie theatre where he took us to watch newsreels of what went on in the world.

I had also learned that Gandhiji stopped the Indian Independence movement during World War II and asked the Indian troops to join the British in the wild forests of Burma and Assam to fight against the Japanese. I remember Unni Maaman and Kesu Maaman, my ammo-omma's brothers returning from the war in their khakis and brown worn out boots. What I remember the best was the canned foods, fish and chicken they brought in their rations. I tasted canned foods for the first time and thought they were salty.

Dad and Ammachi explained to me how the deals for a free India were thwarted by the Muslim groups led by M. Jinnah, who was a good friend of Gandhiji up until then. Jinnah wished to partition the populous subcontinent of India into India and Pakistan. Gandhiji and Jinnah had fought for the freedom alongside each other and along with Pandit Jawaharlal Nehru and Sri. Vallabhai Patel. I could not grasp the depth or the future implications of the discussion at the time.

On August 15th, 1947, India was proclaimed free of the British rule. On the same day the country of Pakistan was formed totally on the fact that the Northwest Territory of India was predominantly Muslim. At the opposite side, in the Northeast corner, the area was declared as East Pakistan, solely based on the fact that the predominant population there was also Muslim.

People took to the streets singing and dancing in celebration of the freedom achieved without bloodshed or war. There were fairs, festivals and parades.

Amongst all the rejoicing, tragedy struck.

In the days immediately following the independence declaration, the Muslims from all over India were moving to Pakistan, while the Hindus from Pakistan were migrating to free India. This resulted in clashes and conflict among the masses, many of whom felt disenchanted with the decision of their leaders. Most of the ordinary people did not care for this mandatory uprooting of their lives and felt betrayed. In Pakistan, entire villages where the Hindus and Sikhs lived were burnt to ashes. The Hindus fleeing from Pakistan were attacked, trains burned and the roads were strewn with the burned and mutilated bodies. The Muslims going to Pakistan were also attacked and beaten to death.

The massive fights that broke out ended with enormous death tolls. I saw some pictures and the photo reels of the bloodshed on the trains and roads that connected the two newly formed nations. The shadow of the conflict fell on both nations. This broke Gandhiji's heart. He tearfully pleaded on cinema screens and on the radio to stop the violence. The Congress party in India formed the Parliament and took measures to unify a country with twenty-eight different languages, each with their own alphabet and grammar, and more than thirty dialects. All the different kingdoms had their own kings, **Maharajas** and that was a big issue that needed resolution. The Rajas were renamed *Rajpramukhs,* and made into figureheads who were allowed to keep their personal assets, and able to oversee local royal functions in each of their states. Some of the politically active Rajas were included in various state assembly or cabinet positions. Whatever land or business they were granted became their own personal assets and were treated as such.

Pandit Jawaharlal Nehru was the first Prime Minister of the newly formed Nation. A few months later, a Hindu Nationalist assassinated Gandhiji. The Nation and the World mourned a great man who led India to freedom without any bloody confrontation with the British and who espoused non-violence as a means to confront the oppressors. Non-violence did not just mean no violence but also non-cooperation with unjust laws in order to overturn them.

The Republic of India was born on January 26th, 1949. I still remember our attending the military parade at the Pangode Military center. The splendour of the multiple colors of the fireworks that burst in the night sky at the Central Stadium in town is unforgettable, not just for the show but also for the sentiments and the gladness of a people free in their own country.

# 19

## A Betrothal and a Betrayal

RAJ WAS BETROTHED to me at the time of my birth.

Actually, we were betrothed to each other before either one was even conceived. Our fathers were good friends. My twenty-seven year-old dad, K. V. Sivaraam, was married to my seventeen-year-old mother, Retnamma, for almost one year when my father's dear friend M. Kesavan Nair who was twenty-four at the time married a fifteen-year-old girl named Meenakshy Kutty.

In our community there is a very sweet custom honoring newly-weds. Close relatives and close family friends invite the couple to their homes for a feast and something sweet is always served on this occa-sion. My ammoomma invited *Kesavan Maaman*, Kesavan Uncle, and his wife over for a congratulatory dinner. The story goes that after the dinner Kesavan Maaman said to my father, "Eday, hey man, if I have a boy and you have a girl, let us get them married."

My dad agreed. As they wished, Kesavan Maaman and Meenakshy Kutty had a son the next year, and a year and a half later, I was born. Their plans came true. The boy-child was the older by twenty months, which is what they wished for in an arranged marriage anyway.

Both of our families lived in the same town, and our fathers met for evening walks, and all the time they were plotting their children's future. Both were true leaders and do-gooders in the society, and knew all the movers and shakers in town. They were both quite influential in their own right. We visited each other's homes once in a while and also saw each other at the homes of mutual friends. My earliest pre-school memories include occasions when Kesavan Maaman approached me and called me *Maru-molé*, daughter-in law. When I was three or four years old I loved the attention. At eight and nine years of age I did not relish the attention because of the reaction of my sisters and my cousins who giggled and harassed me. It was quite embarrassing. As soon as I heard his voice I ran and hid in a bedroom or in the kitchen, until he either coaxed me out or left without seeing me. Our fathers' decision certainly played havoc in my life. Yet in my young mind, the idea took hold that his son, Raj, whom I called Balu Chettan, was to be my future husband and his face became enshrined in my heart as well.

When I turned thirteen my relationship to my future father-in-law changed. He entrusted me in errands to be done for him. Raj's family lived in a suburb of Thiruananthapuram called Nemom. The road to Nemom went past my ammoomma's house. When Kesavan Maaman needed prescriptions filled from the drugstore near the hospital he requested I pick up the medicines because the drugstore would close before he left to go home. He took interest in my studies and encouraged me to enroll in additional math and chemistry courses at Victory Tutorial College, a private junior college that he owned. He and my father agreed it would help me achieve better grades, although I was an above average student in school.

Around this time our families saw each other often. My ammoomma was their family doctor. Meenakshy Kutty, who was my *Thankom Maami,* was a regular patient, what with the number of pregnancies she went through.

My being promised to Raj was common knowledge among my friends and colored all my activities in school, at the tennis club, or even in my dance class. My girlfriends spoke of him as my future husband. While I had good friends among the boys in our club or at social gatherings, they knew that I was not approachable. I considered myself special because I was spoken for.

Raj was always in my dreams. We had only spoken to each other on less than a handful of occasions to avoid being the target of teasing by our friends and siblings. But that did not keep me from dreaming of what he would tell me if we ever had a chance to be alone, which did not happen in the early 1950s. And it did not stop me from dreaming of him.

1954, Raj(standing,) and Family

The year I turned sixteen was when Raj started medical school. When I was seventeen I too procured admission to the Trivandrum Medical College. The university policies changed that year and our class was required to do one year of *Pre-medical courses* in the regular undergrad school before going to the Medical College itself.

One evening, on his way home from work, Kesavan Maaman stopped at my doctor ammoomma's house and asked me to register Thankom Maami for her delivery at the Women and Children's Hospital where my ammoomma practiced. Maami was expecting their ninth child. The fact that Maaman had entrusted me with the registration for the delivery room was taken by me as an endorsement of my choice of medicine as a career. I was immensely pleased.

I did as he requested. I reserved a room for Thankom Maami in the *pay-ward*, the private-room-section of the hospital, for the week of her expected delivery date. Three weeks later, when Thankom Maami went into labor, instead of bringing her to be admitted to the hospital, Raj came to pick up my ammoomma for home delivery of the baby. Kesavan Maaman had cancelled the plans for a hospital delivery and had opted for Maami to deliver their ninth child, a boy, at home. Ammoomma went to their house, accompanied by her favorite midwife, Subhadra, for the birth of a baby boy. I clearly remember attending the naming ceremony for him, *Jayan*, a month later.

Then came the time for me to go to the Trivandrum Medical College. My dad insisted as a courtesy and a show of respect to my future father-in-law, I needed to call and notify him of my first day at the medical school. I called Kesavan Maaman at Victory Tutorial College, the private junior college he owned and ran, to give him my good news.

That evening he stopped by the house. "You can't become a doctor," he declared, hugging me close, and with a pat on my head. His voice was unusually firm.

"Why?" I asked. "I thought you knew that I wished to be a doctor when I grew up. I have always talked about following in my doctor ammoomma's footsteps."

"Your maami has nine children. As the oldest daughter-in-law, how can you manage a career in medicine and be a good daughter-in-law?"

I laughed. "You know Maaman; my ammoomma has raised three children and nurtured more than another dozen in this house where I grew up. I am sure I can manage a family and a career. I will always help Maami with the kids, and besides, she has plenty of household help even now."

I knew he was not pleased with my choice, but he did not bring the subject up again with me after that night.

I proceeded to attend Trivandrum Medical College in August 1958.

On a balmy, beautiful evening, two months after I was officially a 'young medico' (as we first year medical students were called), I was busy with a game of tennis with friends at the college grounds. Two courts away, Raj and his friends were also enjoying a good game. Laughter filled the air as the players in different courts commented on the neighboring players, ridiculing one another on a bad serve or chasing after an errant ball, or trying to steal a good ball that came into our court, especially if it was less bald than the ones we ourselves were using.

I looked up, and on the dirt road leading up to the courts, I saw Kesavan Maaman's parked car with Kesavan Maaman himself, and his son-in-law, Radhakrishnan, standing beside it. As soon as my game was over I walked up to them and saw that Thankom Maami and Raj's sister, Ambika, were also sitting in the car. We had a very cordial visit while we waited for Raj to finish his game. Kesavan Maaman gave me a ride back to the women's hostel and drove off, taking Raj with them.

The next evening I was called to the phone at the common hall in my women's hostel, as our dorm was labeled. To my pleasant surprise it was Raj on the line. "Can you meet me in front of the Anatomy Hall after morning dissections?"

I answered, "Yes."

I could not persuade him to tell me what it was about. The call seemed not-so-pleasant anymore.

I had no idea what was so important that Raj had to see me immediately. I kept tossing and turning in bed, which was very unlike me. I usually dozed off the minute my head hit my pillow. It must have been after 3:00 a.m. when I finally fell asleep. When the alarm rang at 6:00 I did not want to wake up. Suddenly I realized I needed to meet Raj later that morning which shocked me out of bed. It was a good thing I did not have time to ponder what he wanted to discuss that morning.

As the first year medical students, we started our day between 7.30 and 8.00 a.m. with two hours of dissecting cadavers. I will never forget the morning our group was identifying muscle groups of the leg, nerve and vessel distributions to each of the legs, at the time. Others had opened the abdomen of their assigned body and the smell of formalin used for preserving the bodies hung on our coats through the rest of the day. The morning break after the dissections usually gave us just enough time to scrub our hands and grab a cup of coffee before we went on to our physiology lectures.

So next morning after the anatomy session, I met Raj on the balcony between the lecture halls.

We had grown up knowing that we were betrothed to each other. While we saw each other at family gatherings, we had never spoken at any length of things that mattered, or even of inconsequential things. We were acutely aware of how the others paid attention to us together.

The only time I had spoken to him was two days after I joined the Medical College when I needed him to do me a favor. My special pair of expensive eyeglasses, a congratulatory gift from Daddy, had been stolen from my book pack at our tennis courts. So, I called Raj at the men's hostel and asked him to please put a notice up on their bulletin board in an effort to find them. Nobody snitches on a fellow who committed such a crime. I knew that. But I had to make an effort. Albeit it was an effort in vain.

Now I was anxious to find out why Raj needed an urgent meeting with me in the middle of a school day.

I was prompt. He was already there waiting, leaning on the half wall of the balcony as I approached. He was not smiling. My heart skipped a beat. He looked so young and the look on his face was too serious on such a young man. After a casual hello, he got straight to the point.

"I don't know what your thoughts are on the subject, but I grew up thinking I am supposed to marry you." He spoke in a tentative voice, while he searched my face intently for my reaction. "But now, my father tells me that I am not to see you or have anything to do with you. Last evening when my parents came to pick me up, they took me all the way back home to Nemom, to tell me that."

I was in shock. No words came to reply to this bomb he had

dropped on me. But I said a silent prayer to Lord Krishna as I often did when facing difficulties.

*Just two years previously, Kesavan Maaman had pushed to have us photographed as fiancés and even the last time I saw him he had called me 'maru-mol,'(meaning daughter-in-law.)*

1955  Shaku and Raj, first photo together.

"Don't you have anything to say?" I heard his words, echoing in a distance. I was in a trance, and his face seemed distal and hazy.

"I have always thought that you would be my husband one day."

*I did not tell him how he permeated all my dreams, and how my friends made my days intolerable with their teasing every time our paths crossed. I did not tell him how I dreamed of our wedding day when I would place a garland of flowers on his neck to accept him as my husband, amid live music from a wedding band who played clarinet and drums loud enough to drown the cheers of both our families.*

*I did not know for sure until that day how he thought of me as his choice for a partner in his life. I was relieved.*

"And now you say that it will not happen?" I asked, overwhelmed and nervous.

"I always thought of you as my future bride, also," he continued. "What are we going to do now?"

"I don't think I can imagine a life without you." I blurted out.

"Maybe we can meet later after classes and discuss this further?" His voice broke.

"There is nothing to discuss. I am quite sure that you are the one I want to marry. After eighteen years of brainwashing, I am not going to give you up now." I know I must have come off as 'bold' for a young lady. But appearances did not matter at a time like this. It was our future at stake. It was my Raj whom I would lose if I got timid, and I was not known to be a timid one.

"As long as I know this is what you want too, I can make plans for our future regardless of what my father wants. They, my parents, don't have the right to change their minds after all these years." He too was adamant.

So started our relationship, our romance. In a town where even newlyweds went places with a chaperone in the first few weeks, it was unheard of in our families and in our own community, that young people met and dated in 1958.

My dad seemed surprised when I told him what had happened. He said I should take it easy, concentrate on my studies and allow fate to take its course. "You have plenty of time before you graduate," he said. "After you both finish school, Kesavan Maaman will change his mind. I am sure he will let Balu (that was Raj's pet name) marry you then." Eternal optimist that he was, he did not know Raj well enough nor how he would not be able to ignore a challenge and leave things alone.

*In 1958, the day his father prohibited him from seeing me, Raj declared his love for me. I was seventeen and Raj nineteen, and we pledged our love to each other on a balcony near the Anatomy lab in our Medical College, where we were both medical students at the time.*

We were devastated. But where I was sad and frustrated, Raj's frustration turned to anger and a stubborn determination to oppose his father's dictum. I spoke to my parents and Ammachi about the problem and they advised me to be patient and to give Raj's father time to cool off.

To discourage Raj from seeing me, his father took him out of the men's hostel and so Raj became a day scholar. This was difficult on him because he took a bus to town from his home in the suburbs of Thiruananthapuram and transferred to another bus to get to the Medical College campus and the hospitals he rotated in. He had difficulty reaching morning rounds at the hospital so his professor phoned Raj's father to notify him about Raj's tardy attendance. So, with his father's permission, Raj started driving the family car to get to his classes in time.

Raj would meet me on campus after classes. We would walk along the college gardens and sit on the garden benches to talk about our future together. Nothing about this time was easy. Kesavan Maaman had many friends among the doctors and office staff. By the time Raj and I returned to my ladies' hostel after our evening walks, Kesavan Maaman received reports of our rendezvous. When Raj returned home he was not only chastised, but received corporal punishment for his disobedience. Kesavan Maaman did not hesitate to swish a twig on Raj's back to express his anger for disobeying him. But the more severe the punishment, the more insistent was Raj to see me. He was caught between his father's dictum and his love for me. At eighteen, I was not very wise. My only aim was to reduce his pain. But to do this I needed to be with him, and I tried to spend as many evenings as I could with him when he came to the Medical College campus.

On Saturday evenings there was always screening of English movies on the college lawn. We saw the Three Stooges and Charlie Chaplin movies. We couldn't go to town to a regular movie theater for fear of flaunting our love in public, and knowing this would be disrespectful to Kesavan Maaman, even if Raj was angry at him.

In those days it was unheard of in our community that teenagers would date, or even go to a movie without a chaperone. In order to keep peace at home we only met each other on the college campus. I was happy to see Raj, but miserable about all the rules we were breaking. My position put my parents at odds with their old friends, too, which also made me uncomfortable.

A tumultuous two years followed. Our romance flourished despite road blocks set up by Kesavan Maaman. The sad part was that we never heard an explanation of why our betrothal was cancelled. My becoming a doctor was a lame excuse, and I knew that. I found out much later how, despite Thankom Maami's pleadings, Kesavan Maaman refused to accept that Raj was in love with me.

He took Raj out of the men's hostel. He ended up traveling long distances to attend classes as a day scholar, often changing two buses to make it to clinical sessions at ungodly hours and sleeping in a friend's hostel room when the night classes ran late and the buses to town were not running anymore.

Raj picked up the gauntlet his dad threw in front of him. He insisted we meet in the evenings after classes, or see Saturday evening movies on the college lawn together. Being a socially prominent person, Kesavan Maaman's friends in the college offices and campus continued to alert him whenever we were seen together, and every time Maaman found out he made life miserable for Raj.

During the next two years I was able to convince my family that Raj was the one who I wanted to marry.

[Our love story was included in my previous memoir, **Song of the Mountains, My Pilgrimage to Maa Ganga**.]

## TRIVANDRUM MEDICAL COLLEGE

1958. Trivandrum Medical College.

1970.   Balcony, Trivandrum Medical College

2010. Trivandrum Medical College.

Raj and I visited the school for the last time in 2010.

All this came to a sad end when Raj's father died of a sudden illness the same year Raj completed his final year in medicine.

One morning in early November 1960, Raj phoned me at my woman's hostel to say that Kesavan Maaman was admitted at the Medical College Hospital with bleeding in his gums. He also told me I should not go to visit his father at the hospital.

I honored his request although I wished badly to go and be by Kesavan Maaman's bedside. Seeing my agony over the situation, my friend Padma stopped by the hospital to inquire about his diagnosis. She found Kesavan Maaman's bone marrow had shut down, Aplastic anemia, versus an acute leukemia were the two reasons considered for his bleeding problem. For the next week my many friends took turns visiting him and kept me apprised of his progress, or the lack thereof, as it turned out. At the end of the brief week-long illness, Kesavan Maaman passed away at the young age of forty-seven. He left behind a wife who was barely thirty-eight years old and ten children, the youngest ten months old, and the oldest, Raj, just finishing his medical college curriculum and not yet earning a salary.

The consensus was that Kesavan died of Aplastic anemia; most likely due to a reaction to medicine he had taken containing a heavy metal component.

Raj, my Balu Chettan, graduated the next year.

The ultimate betrayal lay in the fact that Kesavan Maaman died without giving me an opportunity to show him I truly loved him and his family as my own. He died without giving me a chance to convince him that I would be the best daughter-in-law he and his wife could have, and how as a practicing physician I would still have time to include my husband's siblings as my own, because I knew that was the right way to be.

Thinking back on that time still chokes me up. After his father died, Raj, as the oldest son had to step up and perform his father's cremation rituals. Raj was twenty-one years old and weighed eighty-two pounds. My heart broke to watch him as he stood stiff as a stick, defiant against the challenge thrown to him by fate.

At that moment I wondered if Raj was thinking about how he did not get to say goodbye to his father because his father was not cognizant in the last four days of his life. Did he regret the fact he had been estranged from his father due to his love for me and for choosing me over his father's love? I watched him through a stream of tears, praying to Lord Krishna to keep him strong, and keep him safe for the day.

I know for certain he was thinking: *'You left me to take care of my 39-year-old mother and eight children, all less than eighteen years of age. You left me with this enormous burden to feed, guide, and raise these young ones while I graduate from a medical college and am without a job or an income.'*

Then the procession of men took his father's body down to the backyard of their property, where the pyre had been prepared for the funeral. Raj was led down by his older cousin and his uncle to light the wooden pyre, including sandalwood. Following tradition and custom, we women did not walk down to witness him light the funeral pyre. The wailing of the women in the house subsided when Raj and the rest of men walked out of our sight. But, when the rising smoke of the fire became visible a few minutes later, the wailing rose again. Raj's mother was strong; holding on to the younger children, she sat crying quietly. But it was the aunts and the ladies among family and friends who wailed. It was not just for the one who had passed. The heartbreaking wail was also for the young widow, and for the young man-boy who would shoulder the burden of a family, in which the youngest of the ten children was a ten-month-old child. How could I ever think of my Raj without seeing that scene in my mind?

I am certain he changed. By then the conflict with his father had defined him as defiant and difficult for a twenty-one-year-old. Now, the added worry of how to earn a living made his approach to life different from anyone in his peer group. Instead of doing a rotating internship that paid a barely mentionable stipend, he accepted a job as 'instructor" in physiology. He did well in his role as teacher and mentor to first and second year medical students, although they were only two or three years younger than he.

Later that year when he earned his license to practice medicine, he started a pharmacy of sorts in the side-yard of his home, which boasted an outer building with storage facilities, and he held a clinic of his own every weekend.

His mother watched all of his earnings and some of her own income from her rice-fields and rental income she received and invested into this clinic. As was the custom, when a patient was seen at the clinic, Raj had to name a price for his services, and after the diagnosis was made he had to charge them for the appropriate medicine he dispensed from his clinic. But his mother deduced after about six months, that Raj's clinic was running low on income because more than half of the patients he examined were relatives or neighbors and he found it difficult to price and collect the money owed from them. So, she took a stand and pressured him to close shop. In many ways he was relieved.

# 20

## Our Love Story Continues

**THE SUDDEN DEPARTURE** of Kesavan Maaman placed the responsibility of the entire family on Thankom Maami. In essence this meant that the bulk of it fell on Raj, as the oldest son, the only bread-winner, and the one with monthly earnings, as meager as that might have been at the time. After graduation, Raj joined the Department of Physiology as an instructor. His hours were regular and he was able to spend more time with his mother and siblings, eight of whom were still living at Hill View.

A few days after the official mourning period following his father's demise Raj called me to resume our romance. I was hesitant because I did not want to offend or hurt his mother. Raj assured me she had nothing against me and that I need not worry. I could hear it in his voice that he needed to speak to me. In that crucial period when his head was reeling with the thought of the duties in front of him, how could I say 'no?'

I did see him and spent evenings with him before he drove back the long distance to his home. Our conversations were solemn, and the elephant in the room—how he alone would support such a large family—was not addressed for a very long time.

After a few months with the eternal optimism and the combined wisdom of Raj at twenty-two years old, and me at twenty years old, we

decided to leave everything status quo, and just work hard for our future. We decided to take it one day at a time, at least until I graduated
from Medical College in two years. Meanwhile we met and walked
whenever Raj could come to the Medical College campus. Slowly but
surely his smile, his wicked sense of humor and the jauntiness in his
steps returned. His support system, besides me, were his close friends
Dr. T.K. Rajan, his classmate of five years and Dr. Radhakrshnan, his
classmate since junior college (over six years), even before he joined
the medical college. Dr. Radhakrishnan was now a fellow instructor in
Physiology. Raj's main confidante, however, was Velayudhan Annan,
his older cousin on his father's side, who had been his lean-on person throughout the conflict with his father because of our romance.
Velayudhan Annan was always there for him.

Somewhere along the way Raj and three of his friends got the idea
to go to the States for post-graduate training. As much as I did not wish
to leave Thiruvananthapuram and my family, I gave in to his reasoning
that with postgraduate training under our belts, we would have the
prestige to attract a better paying patient population which would enable us to provide for the family. After much coaxing and arguments
back and forth, I went along when Raj took his ECFMG entrance exam
for job-seeking physicians in the States and when he sent applications
to different hospitals in America.

Meanwhile he found out that his mother did not have anything
against me. She had known me all my life. Raj, being her oldest son
and the only breadwinner after his father passed away at the age of
forty-seven years, she acquiesced to his wishes and gave us her blessings to get married.

*Shaku weds Raj, January 21ˢᵗ, 1963*

Two years later we got married at the Devi temple by the Shankumugham beach, in Thiruvananthapuram.

The sun shone bright, the sound of the waves pounding the shore was loud, and the people gathered even louder. My grandmother, my parents, aunts, uncles, sisters, and brother were present. Raj's mom, all nine siblings, two brothers-in-law, and cousins, were gathered at the front yard of the temple. Under a portico roofed with tiles, and surrounded by jasmine garlands, we were wed. Of course, his father was not there because he had passed away three years prior, before he witnessed his firstborn son, Raj, become a doctor. That had been a father's dream, unfulfilled.

The Malayalee marriage ceremony is the shortest of all Hindu marriage ceremonies. It is more of a social custom than a religious function. All the religious prayers and blessings are done ahead of time at a temple service. The social commitments made by the bride and groom to each other form the gist of the wedding ceremony.

In the front yard of the temple, a *mandapam* or gazebo was set up and decorated with garlands of jasmine flowers. A wooden plank covered by white cotton cloth was placed in the center of the gazebo, and an oil lamp lit to the right of this seat. In front of the lamp, a mound of rice grain, a sheaf of coconut flowers and a bunch of fresh fruit, all representing abundance, were placed. Incense sticks were lit, and lively music with three men on drums, one on clarinet and another one playing the flute resounded in the temple yard. The hot sun, the aroma of the flowers and the incense, and the loud rhythmic music set a surreal atmosphere that morning. In the absence of his own father, Raj's uncle led him by hand around the mandapam and seated him on the wooden seat. Accompanied by loud music of the live orchestra, my father led me to the mandapam, and seated me to the left of Raj.

The family and friends gathered around us as I stood up and placed a garland of roses on Raj's neck in a symbol of choosing him as my husband. He reciprocated, placing a rose-garland on my neck. Next, Raj tied a gold leaf pendant called **Thali**, strung on a yellow thread, already blessed in front of the goddess Parvathi, the main deity at this temple. We exchanged gold signet rings, his carrying my name engraved on it and mine carrying his name. He smiled, since we both knew we did not need these to lock our lives together forever. The last item in the wedding was the gifting of new clothes by Raj to me. It consisted of a complete set of clothes for me, including a new pure silk saree, blouse, and even a matching underskirt for the saree. This represented a promise by the bridegroom to support the bride all her life. Once I accepted his gift, we stood together facing family and friends to accept their congratulations and their blessings.

After our wedding, I left my ammoomma's home and went to Raj's home accompanied by my new family. Raj's siblings ranged from twenty-two years to three years of age. We had to decide who rode in the car with us for the half-hour car ride. The younger four kids and one niece entered the car we were riding in... They were truly excited to sit by me, their new *Chechi*, older sister.

A new bride entering the house is considered to be the Lekshmi of the home. Lekshmi is the Goddess of good luck, wealth and happiness. When Raj and I arrived at the house, Thankom Maami, my mother-in-law, had a "reception kit" for the bride all ready. Raj's sister, Ambika, picked up a pot of red-colored water with kum-kum powder added to it and flowers floating in it. She held the pot alongside a lit lamp with a cotton wick. Ambika then waved this holy combination around my head and torso three times, stepped on to the lawn, and turned the whole thing upside down on to the sandy yard in a gesture to grab any unwanted spirits who wished to enter the house with me, the new daughter of the family.

Following this, Baby Chechi, Raj's cousin's wife, handed me a brass oil lamp with a lit wick shining an auspicious light on me. I walked slowly up to the front doorway, protecting the flame dancing in the wind. I entered my new home, placing my right foot forward. Having been cleared of all bad vibes, I was led to the pooja room where I placed the lamp in front of the altar in the room. My first job was a holy act of making Raj's house my own.

My husband's house had a name: "Hill View." On a clear day, from the rear of the house you could see the *Mookkunni mala,* meaning 'the hill with three peaks.'

This was supposed to be the happiest day of my life. While we laughed and carried on with Raj's siblings, who ran all around trying to please me, I felt the disapproval of Raj's dead father looming over us like a low dark cloud. When I mentioned it to Raj, he said I should not worry about it because the only thing that mattered was that his mom, Thankom Maami loved me, and to remember that he was glad we'd finally gotten married. As is customary, my new mother-in-law even had three sets of saree outfits with matching blouses for me to change into when I arrived home. My home. The Chenthitta house was not my home anymore. As much as I wished to be Raj's wife, the shock of this realization was a bit too much for me. The separation from my family affected me more than I expected or realized. The sight of the sad faces of my ammoomma, Ammachi, mom, dad, and my sisters as we left the temple after our wedding, haunted me.

In the late afternoon we retired to our room for a while. After all those years of anxiety, hoping, conflicts and more tension, we were finally together, away from the hustle and bustle of family and friends, and we had a few moments together. Suddenly I burst into tears. Raj soothed my tears and hugged me close. He convinced me to take a nap with him.

When we woke up a couple of hours later Raj declared that we were going to town to see my ammoomma. He said that would appease my worry and make me feel better. He drove me to town and when we arrived at my ammoomma's, the house was dark, and the lamps were not lit, and no one was chanting the prayers at dusk. It was more like a house of mourning. Yes, they had lost me to Raj's family, but this was sadder than I expected. As soon as Raj and I walked in, the mood changed. Lamps were lit, prayers done, and sweet snacks and payasam served. We both sat on Ammoomma's bed to visit with her. Ammachi and my cousins gathered around us. Shanthi was not there because she had moved to Tanzania with her husband, and they had not come to our wedding because they were expecting their first baby in six weeks.

If it was up to me I would have wanted to go see my dad also. Yet, I knew it was too much to ask. I telephoned Dad and Mom from my ammoomma's house and spoke to them. They were happy to hear my voice. If they were disappointed we did not stop by their house, they did not show it in their voices. I knew they were being kind to me.

When we returned to my new home I was in a much better state of mind. It made me feel good that despite all the demands of his family Raj recognized how hard it was for me to leave my family and tried to ease my separation from them. Although I was not moving too far away from home, the fact of my new commitment to my husband's family loomed ahead and was messing with my young head.

Our wedding was on a Monday in January 1963. It was only two years and two months after his father's demise, so we had not planned on going away on a honeymoon and leaving his mother, a young widow at forty, with seven of Raj's siblings still under fifteen years old. Two days later, on Wednesday morning, Raj decided we should all go to Kanyakumari, the beach resort at the very southern tip of the Indian peninsula to celebrate our wedding. Being a last-minute decision, we could only get three rooms in *The Kerala House,* a hotel set-up run by the Kerala Government. Packed into three cars, we all went——the newly-weds, two sisters and their husbands, all seven younger siblings, a niece, and a baby nephew. With only three rooms, Raj and I took one and the rest of the family shared two rooms. For years the whole family would joke about how we shared our honeymoon with the family, and how we stole a room all to ourselves, leaving the rest in two crowded rooms.

The unique feature of this beach was that the waters of the Arabian Sea from the west, the Indian Ocean from the South, and the Bay of Bengal from the east roll in to merge and mingle, offering wide sandy beaches for people to enjoy. This is one of only six spots in the world where you can see the sun rise from the waters in the East and set into the sea in the West.

The air was warm, the waves wild as ever, and we had fun with all the little ones in the sand and sun. At the bathing Ghat the waters flow in from all three directions and the bathers are somewhat protected by rock formations all around. Thankom Maami refused to come into the water.

A temple dedicated to Kanya Kumari Devi, the virgin Goddess stands on the shores of this special place. At sundown we walked over to the temple and offered fruit and flowers, along with prayers to make us strong to take care of this brood of loved ones that divine fate had placed in our sole care. My tears flowed freely even as I was smiling at Molly, Raj's three-year-old sister, who was perched on Raj's shoulders. It was clearer than ever—he was my only love, my Raj.

Soon I realized why my family was anxious about my wedding. Raj, at twenty-five, was solely responsible for the future of these seven young lives. I was not yet practicing medicine, looking at another year of rotating internship before I could get my license to practice. Seeing the responsibility I was undertaking alongside Raj at such a young age, my parents and Ammoomma were genuinely concerned for me.

Looking back I think I really understood Raj's mindset when he decided to go to the United States for further training and to specialize in Internal Medicine. The better trained and experienced he and I would become, the better prepared we would be to take care of this big family that we had inherited. I can also see how we were both deciding on these plans based on a platform of love for our young family, and not out of a feeling of obligation.

The added tension was the decision to go or not go to the States hanging over us. It was a very good thing that our daily life was so hectic that we did not have much time to worry about the impending separation.

Our home at *Hill View* did not have running water. Early in the morning a lady came to draw enough well water to fill a huge brass pot placed over a stove, lit with dry coconut palm leaves and dry wood. When the water was hot it was mixed with cold water in buckets and used for our baths. Although it was a warm country the weather in the early mornings was cool enough to warrant warm water for bathing. So it was that there was a long line of us waiting in queue to take our baths. Then there was the rush of getting the four girls and one teenage boy to finish breakfast and be packed into the car, all the while trying to get ourselves ready for work. We dropped them all at their schools in town, and then rushed off to the medical campus. Raj was an instructor in physiology, and I was rotating through all the various departments for my internship. After school the five children walked over to my oldest sister-in-law Ambika's house in the city. When we were back from the college campus we met them there. Because Ambika had city water it was easier to have them take baths and change clothes before we returned home to Hill View.

Whenever I brought up the subject of Raj's trip to the United States, he deflected the topic immediately by telling me that I would join him in January 1964, as soon as I completed my internship. He also reminded me that his uncle had agreed to come stay with his mother and the children while we were gone. And, we were planning to be away for just five years, until he completed his postgraduate training. His words did not allay my fears, yet I knew I did not have any choice but to agree to his plans. I understood how strongly responsible he felt about the financial stability of the whole family, especially the little ones. He convinced me that our practice of medicine would be up to date and greatly improved, and life would be much easier once we had flourishing practices. Yet, every time the subject came up, I burst into tears. I was the emotional one, and tears fell easily, whether I encountered good or bad news. And this was a mixture of both.

Two months after we wed, Raj received offers from a few hospitals in the States, for rotating internships, the first step toward higher education. After deep discussions, he chose McNeal Hospital in Berwyn, Illinois. His classmate and friend, Dr. Joseph Eipe, was doing an internship at the same hospital and Raj would start his internship on July 1, 1963. When he had a chance to apply and get selected for a rotating internship at MacNeal Memorial Hospital in Illinois, he decided he could not pass up the opportunity of being trained in the States. At the end of June 1963 Raj left our home in *Hill View* and travelled to Berwyn, Illinois, leaving me to complete my internship in Trivandrum.

It was hard on us both to be separated. We did not have a choice.

During that time I stayed on with his mother and eight of his siblings. As much as I missed my ammoomma and my parents, I felt an obligation to stay with Thankom Maami, because it was the right thing to do. Especially after what Raj and I had gone through to overcome obstacles and be united as husband and wife.

We had a Dalmatian, Laika, who had a playful pleasant disposition and did not pick up on my dour moods or Raj's excitement about his overseas trip. She was named after the first dog that went to space in the Russian Rocket ship Sputnik II in 1957. Raj used to spend a lot of time with her, and she loved it. After Raj left, Laika was still a happy dog, playing with the children and following them around. Once in a while she came into our room looking for Raj but left as soon as I paid some attention to her.

We also had a second older dog, Sabu. He was a classic Alsatian, who was stand-offish with most of us, but loved playing with the children, and allowed them to ride him. The littlest one, Molly, just three years old, even cuddled by him when she was tired. He especially loved her because she often poured out her milk for him to drink. His fierce bark was ever more protective than his appearance which was intimidating by the sheer size--tall and husky as he was. He followed Raj inside and outside the house. Sabu was heartbroken when Raj left. After Raj's departure, I shared my room with Chaku, my sister-in-law, still a high school student. Sabu barked at her as if to question why she was in Raj's bed. He sniffed at the clothes Raj had worn before he left and moaned non-stop whenever he came into my room. That would set me off in tears again.

Exactly one week after Raj left, Sabu was found lying still on the garage floor, lifeless from a broken heart. He had played with the children and eaten a good dinner the previous night. To find his still body the next morning was quite a shock to Thankom Maami, myself, and the children, We cremated him in a plot next to my father-in-law's cremation plot and planted a mango tree over the spot in his memory. The coconut palm that was planted over Kesavan Maaman's cremation site three years before had already grown over six feet tall.

That night I returned to my room to prepare to watch over the kids, their homework, and their vaccination schedules. After my family duties were complete, I took out the papers to prepare for my tests that I had to take before applying for Residency Program in the Chicago area.

*1963 Family photo. Chenthitta House*
*Standing: Raj fifth from left. my dad is second from right.*
*Sitting: Ammachi is third from left. Ammoomma fourth,*
*and myself fifth from left.*
*My Mom is seated first from right.*

Photo # 21.     *1963, Hill View Family photo.*
*Standing: Raj second from left.*
*Sitting: Shaku second from left. Thankom Maami in the center.*
*Raj's siblings, one brother-in-law, and his cousin and family.*

# 21

## Major Life Changes

**I, DR. SHAKUNTALA** Rajagopal, was now a full-fledged adult.

I was married with children, and a dog, and a job that amounted to full time and a half, being on call three or four nights a week. The work involved long hours in the patient wards, taking histories, doing physical examinations, and ordering relevant laboratory tests or x-ray studies to aid in the diagnosis of different conditions. At patient rounds, the attending physician came to examine the patient. At that time I presented all the findings and gave my impression of the patient's diagnosis. Most of the cases were straightforward and the diagnosis I made came close to, if not on the dot, of the patient's true condition. When I missed a finding or a clue in their family history or physical examination, most of the attending physicians were merciless in their critique and did not hesitate to point out my mistake in front of other interns and residents. Initially this bothered me and the other interns. But eventually we developed thick skins and took the critique in stride. After all, taking care of the patient was our primary goal, not appeasing our ego.

Many elderly patients filled the medical wards. They were very thankful when we detected the cause for their suffering and were able to help them heal.

In the maternity ward there was quite a bit of anxiety, because the life and well-being of the mother and baby combined were at stake, which made all changes from the norm inherently tense issues. Because we were at a university hospital in addition to being a city hospital, many of the OB-GYN patients were non-compliant to their doctors' advice and came only when their conditions were really acute. When we worked these wards, we were on our feet all of the twenty-four hour shift, and often scrubbed for surgery with one of the attending.

The experience we gained in taking care of the various problems helped us grow strong in our knowledge and our confidence. My only regret was, I would soon leave my hometown and these people behind, but I knew my priority was my husband and I was already yearning to be with him. That topped all other concerns.

Yet, the fact of leaving my ammoomma, dad, mom, ammachi and my siblings nagged at my conscience and gave me sleepless nights. Now the list of concerns grew longer. Thankom Maami and the little ones at Hill View were also my concern. The more time I spent with them the harder it was to leave them. Raj had said repeatedly, "We will only be gone for five years. That will pass so quickly, and we will be back before you know it."

I knew I was helpless in that situation. I had to go.

I prepared for the ECFMG exams (Equivalency Certificate for Foreign Medical Graduates). I needed to pass those exams to apply for Residency positions in the United States. The closest testing center was in Madras, our neighboring state to the east. My dad and I took a train to Madras so I could take the test. I talked to my dad about my concerns of missing everybody. He reassured me of the importance of my duty to join my husband, which I wanted to do anyway, and I should trust God to help me do the right thing. He fully believed God would take care of me wherever I went. He did express his wish regarding our return after post-graduate training—that Raj and I should start a hospital where a portion of the medical services would be dedicated to free treatment for the poor people who could not afford proper medical care. I too had those good intentions when I set off to improve myself and my doctor skills in the wide, wild, west.

I would have loved to join my ammoomma in her medical practice and assume it when she retired. I was raised a dutiful daughter, but even more to be a responsible and dutiful adult. For this reason I made sure I stood by my dear husband to help him perform his man-of-the-house duties for his mother. As much as I felt safe and comfortable in my life in Thiruananthapuram, I knew my **dharma**, or customary duty, directed me to join him in America and help him work toward our dream of owning our medical practice. I realized later that despite our young ages of twenty-five and twenty-three years old we made some momentous decisions in 1963 which changed our lives forever.

Many of my cousins and friends could not understand why I would hesitate to leave India. Some of them told me that given the chance they would not hesitate for one moment to go abroad for higher studies. However at that point in our lives none of us were even thinking of leaving our motherland to make a life anywhere else in the world. Free India was only sixteen years old versus thousands of years of ancient civilization, with that background and with the newly established progress independent India was experiencing, none of us had any idea of leaving the country for good. All we wished was to gain more knowledge and experience in order to make our future and our family's future prosperous and secure.

# 22

## My New World

MAJOR LIFE CHANGES often come without notice, and many times against our hopes and dreams. The only way to survive what life throws at you is to face it directly, to accept and adapt to it, or change what you cannot accept to the best of your ability. Some changes will take longer than you like, but eventually you will get a handle on the situation. Faith in God, faith in ourselves, and faith in our ability to change will always help. How you build your faith is influenced by your family, your community and even the country in which you live. In the end, your faith depends on what you have vested in it, as well as your life's outcome.

### *My Journey*

My journey of 10,000 miles began with 10,000 blessings.

In October 1963, I went on a pilgrimage with my mother and father to the temples they had frequented throughout our state of Kerala in South India. This was their way of preparing me for my journey the following January to join my husband, Raj, who was already doing his internship in faraway Chicago. Both Mom and Dad were religious and spiritual people who felt strongly that I needed to travel to those temples in Kerala where the deities were important to them. I was to gather the blessings of those special deities before I set out on my journey.

The blessings offered me a sense of security for my trip. If at twenty-three years old, the farthest you have travelled alone in your life, without another family member accompanying you, is a bus trip to the tennis club two and a half miles away, then 10,000 miles from home was an awfully long way to go.

I could not go any farther from my home, anywhere on this earth, if I'd wanted to. My hometown Trivandrum, India, and Chicago, Illinois are on the opposite sides of the earth. If I bored a tunnel straight through from Thiruananthapuram, I would land less than a half inch to the west and barely three inches due south of Chicago, according to my one-foot world globe.

In my estimation I tried to quantify the number of blessings I carried from the Gods I visited and the people who blessed me.

Packing for my trip to Chicago, the very first items that my mother and I placed at the bottom of my suitcase were sachets of prasadams, blessed offerings of dried sandalwood paste, from the temple at Guruvayoor, dedicated to Lord Krishna. This was one of the twelve temples we visited as part of my pilgrimage. When my father, mother and I, along with my sister and her baby boy, arrived at Guruvayoor, 159 miles north of Trivandrum, about three or four hundred devotees were already pushing and shoving to get a glimpse of the idol of Lord Krishna. We waited in line for over an hour before we finally made it to the sanctum sanctorum. I chanted my Krishna prayers as I watched the priest decorate the idol of Lord Krishna for the pooja services at noon. He covered the idol from head to toe in a thick layer of sandalwood paste. To make the paste, sticks of sandalwood were ground on the surface of a stone mortar, and collected into bowls with reverence by the priest's helpers. I had a feeling of warmth and gladness as I witnessed such a true labor of love and devotion.

Floral garlands made from white jasmines, bright red hibiscus petals, green Tulsi leaves and orange-red ixora blossoms were reverently hung/draped over his chest. Vibrant gold ornaments were added to adorn him from the crown on his head, large studs on his ears, four or five long chains hanging from his neck, bangles on both forearms, an arinjanam or waist links, complete with gold anklets on both legs. The adornments stayed on Lord Krishna until after the evening pooja services.

The flickering flames of over a hundred oil lamps cast a surreal aura in the sanctum. The aroma of incense sticks, the chanting of the thousand names of Lord Krishna by the priests, and the ringing of about a dozen brass bells transported me to a place where I felt the blessings emanate from the idol of Lord Krishna, thus dissipating any timidity in my leaving home for the first time. We waited in the adjacent rest house during the hot afternoon.

The evening services were uplifting with chanting of prayers by devotees, blessing of fruit and food items in front of the idol of Lord Krishna, and pooja rituals to honor the Lord. Dressed in saffron and red silks and adorned by gold ornaments and long flower garlands, the Deity exuded unbelievable strength which built confidence in me that I could travel forward alone, though I would not truly be alone.

After the evening services the sandalwood paste was removed and distributed to devotees as blessed offerings called prasadams. My parents and I waited our turn to receive our shares. We brought the sandalwood paste home and dried it in the sun into a light golden-yellow powder for long-term preservation. This was then packed into small sachets to travel with me to the United States. Later, when I wished to invoke the blessings of Lord Krishna of Guruvayoor, I would reconstitute a pinch of the sandalwood powder, using a drop of water, and then wear the paste on my forehead as a symbol of the Lord's blessing.

In our Hindu household, the religious fervor ranged from an occasional temple visit by my grandmother, to daily offerings of flowers to the nearest Devi Temple by my mother who said a prayer with every breath she took. My father's practice had an air of great sophistication as a devout follower of a guru who guided him and us in the path toward the knowledge of God. I leaned more toward the ritualistic practice of my religion; the structured life suited me well. I took comfort in my prayers yielding results, and yet when what I prayed for did not come true, the Gods were my comfort in handling my disappointment.

So, it was only natural that we packed the ashes from the Ganesha homam, a prayer ritual where pieces of coconuts with the shell on, various fruits and flowers, and ghee, clarified butter, were offered in a wood burning fire in front of Lord Ganesha. While the blazing fire consumed the various offerings, we chanted special prayers to Lord Ganesha to propitiate him. He was the deity who removed all obstacles when one set out on a trip, took an exam or started a new endeavour. Of course, I needed his blessings for my new life in the States.

One week before I set out for Chicago in January 1964 I performed another prayer ritual of Ponkala, to please Goddess Lekshmi, the goddess of health, wealth and happiness. I did this at my Maami's house. I called my mother-in-law *Maami*, meaning aunty in Malayalam, my native tongue. After my marriage my Maami's house was also home to Raj and me. I had stayed on with my maami for the next seven months even after my husband Raj had left for Chicago.

For the Ponkala prayer, I cooked rice in milk and water in our frontyard on a makeshift fireplace made up of three piles of bricks. The distance between the three piles, each about five bricks high, was determined by the size of the glazed ceramic pot that I was using. A fire was made in the center with dry coconut-palm-leaves and some firewood. While the rice cooked, I chanted prayers to Goddess Lekshmi. The blazing fire consumed any bad vibes or spirits that hovered over me. In time, the wood-burning fire was doused by the milk and rice boiling over from the cooking pot. Symbolically, even as my wishes boiled over, this was also a gesture of food offering to the Bhoomi Devi, Goddess Earth. The bonus was that I collected double blessings from the Goddesses, Lekshmi Devi and Bhoomi Devi, to carry with me over the oceans that I had to cross on my trip to Chicago.

We Hindus know that there is only one God, but each time the Lord appears on earth to help the 'good' triumph over 'evil,' the form in which the Lord appears is revered, temples are built in his or her name, and each deity blesses us to make different facets of a person strong.

Then came the goodbyes. In the last week of my stay at home, I bade farewell to many uncles and aunts, cousins and second cousins of my parents, all with vested interest in my success in America. I was the first one from our extended family to travel so far from home, especially to the new world. I bent down and touched the feet of each family elder. The act of touching the feet of an elder signifies a show of respect for their age, maturity, and divinity in them, and at the same time it was to seek their blessing for my upcoming trip, but more so for my journey into a new life. When you touch the feet of an elder and then place your fingers in blessing to your own forehead, you are paying reverence to the God power within that being, and evoking their power for your own benefit. Each of them in turn placed both palms on my shoulders to confer their blessings on me. Some smiled, and some cried, and one great-aunt, Thankamoni Maami, sobbed so hard she could not complete her act of blessing me.

To voluntarily pay homage to another is to empower that God-power in both parties. To be compelled to do so, if you were one of those who questioned this practice, would be ineffective and unthinkable.

If each showered a hundred blessings, I am certain that I collected at least a thousand blessings. Then, of course, there were blessings showered by my immediate family, starting with Mother and Father, and my maternal aunt, Ammachi, who had a bigger role in raising me than my own mother did. My Valiyachan, Ammachi's husband, gave me five hundred blessings, I am sure. He really did not want me to go so far away.

My ammoomma's blessings should have counted for at least a thousand blessings on their own. As I bent down to receive her blessing, she told me, "Remember all that I have taught you. Even as you reach for the skies, keep your feet solidly on the ground." She knew that I had a streak of come-what-may attitude from my father.

My mother's brother, 'Denti-maaman,' was a dentist and my maaman, or uncle; he gave me another five hundred blessings. His wife, my ammavi, was only six years my senior, and she not being a true 'elder' could only be counted for a hundred.

My mother-in-law, Thankom-maami, showered more than a thousand blessings, I am certain. "Ente cherukkane nokkikonam," ("Watch over my boy,") she pronounced. She was happy and relieved that finally I would go over and take care of her son, her first-born. Along with her blessings, she showered me with her unconditional love--love to last for a lifetime, for Raj and me, and for our progeny to come.

I carried all of ten thousand, and maybe more, blessings that were bestowed upon me as I left my home in India for a new life with my bridegroom from whom I had been separated by the seven seas for over seven months.

Once all the packets of prasadams were packed, the clothes, the books, and, above all, my cachet of spices were placed in the box. The cardamom pods, cumin seeds, cloves, nutmeg and fennel would ensure the authenticity of my South Indian cooking that I was prepared to do.

If I knew then that I would not step into a temple ground for over seven and a half years, and that I would be all alone for my evening prayers for most of my life, I wonder if I would have left the safe haven I had known. It is good that I did not know. For, even if I protested, my destiny was beyond my control.

Fifty years later, I still remember how heavy my heart felt to leave my ammoomma and everyone else, but also how the parcel of their blessings acted as an umbrella that raised me in the wind and wafted me over the waters, as a spiritual parachute that assured my smooth landing on new ground.

On my last night at home I sobbed on my mom's shoulder. "I can't leave all of you."

She replied with dry eyes and a firm voice, "Karayathe ponnu-molé," ("Don't cry my golden daughter"), you will see your dear husband, Balu (Raj's nickname) soon. Your place is with him. We will be all right."

All blessings come with strings attached. When I was blessed by my loved ones, my father, mother, ammoomma, maami, they also transferred their power and their past on to me. In accepting their blessings, I felt it was essential to carry on their legacy and the work bestowed upon me by the broad, but often tired, shoulders who carried the burdens before me.

But despite the blessings and despite the empowerment, I felt totally lost and alone in a new country. As much as I was happy to see my husband after such a long time, I miss the many people who surrounded me every day, and the loneliness seemed almost insurmountable at the time.

The purpose of the journey will always color the experiences of the traveler. Being that my one and only aim was to join my love at the other side of the world, love colored all my experiences as the traveler.

What I did not know then was how a journey is not a trip. A trip starts from the point of departure and ends at the point of arrival. In my journey, the point of departure was not a clean break, I imported the sum of my life along for the ride. It was with me when I reached my 'destination.'

My journey had just begun.

# 23

## End of a Long Flight to U.S.A.

ON JANUARY 30, 1964, I landed in New York City, where the welcoming torch of the Statue of Liberty glistened in the evening light as my TWA flight descended from the skies. I would have totally missed the sight if it was not for the kind flight attendant who woke me up to sign some custom forms for entering the country. Seeing how deep in sleep I was, she took the liberty to fill the entry form with information from my ticket and passport. After I signed the form I turned to look out my window and was greeted by the sight of Lady Liberty raising her torch in welcome and offering hope to all who came to her. This flooded my head with excitement. All the dreams I had with Raj about the post graduate training in the U.S.A., and our hope of returning home to India and living a good life with our parents and siblings, and the medical practice we wished to have there made my eyes misty and blurred my vision for a minute. Nevertheless, our goals were clear in my inner mind.

Customs clearance was a blur, except for the comment the inspecting officer made when he tried to restore the contents of my suitcase to close it: "I would like to meet the person who packed this one so tight."

I think I told him it was my mother with the help from my sister, Shanthi. He must have managed to close it. I was too busy scouring the crowd for Raj. It seemed like an eternity before his broad smile and open arms came into sight. I stopped dragging the heavy suitcase and ran to Raj, my *Balu Chettan.* Before he could hug me I bent down to touch his feet to honor him as my husband and my elder, and to receive his blessing. He stopped short, turned to his friend, George, an intern at a State Hospital in upper New York, and laughed. My greeting evoked laughter from Raj and George because as two young modern physicians in America, they felt the custom was quite antiquated. But not me. I was trying to pay my respects to my husband who I was supposed to "revere as my living God on earth," which is what my mom had told me before I left home. Although many miles separated us from our motherland, my heart and my points of reference about everyday civilities of life remained the same as when I'd left just two days previously. After laughing at my demonstration of respect Raj raised me up and hugged me tight. Tears flowed and I could not see his face clearly. He handed me a handkerchief, *"Mathi. Mathi."* Enough, he said as he helped me wipe my tears. "Hey Penne," he tried to separate me from my tight hold on him, "say hello to George. He drove me here to pick you up." I remembered my manners, turned to George and said, "Hello."

Raj kept teasing me about my tears. He did not see that they were tears of joy at seeing him after seven long months, and tears of relief that at last my feet were on the ground. I had not thought about how I would feel to be airborne that long. It was very restrictive, and although I don't have claustrophobia, I was getting close to it by the end of the flight. The fact that I fell asleep made the last leg of the flight easier on me.

I was happy to see Raj did not lose any weight, despite the fact that he had complained in his letters about how poor his cooking skills were. He looked happy and the welcoming smile on his face reassured me that life was going to be good.

Raj brought a winter coat for me, knowing I had to face the cold winds in Chicago, and that I just had a warm sweater with me. I had not worn any garb as heavy as that black coat ever. I looked at the coats Raj and George were wearing, and saw they too looked heavy. Little did I know how the wicked winter winds would assault the totally tropical being that I was.

We said goodbye to George and walked around to the airport restaurant. "I have a surprise for you," he said as he bought us both donuts and coffee. Carrying the donuts and coffee we walked to the boarding gate for our plane to Chicago. My first bite of the donut was his big surprise for me; the sugary treat totally surprised me. In Kerala, we made a salty snack called *Vada*, which has a hole in the center and is deep fried. Therein the similarity ended. The Vada has chopped onions and curry leaves, ginger, salt and peppercorns added in. Despite the total difference from the Vada, I liked the donut. It is still one of my favorites.

Seated comfortably at the gate, we held hands and spoke of how we had missed each other, and filled in the news of how we fared without each other in those long months apart. Every few minutes I touched his face to make sure I was really by his side. In the seven months apart, he had changed. When he left our home in India, he was quite slender. He used to comb his dark black hair up and back, but being thick, wavy and heavy, a few strands always fell over his eyes giving him a boyish look. I noticed he had parted his hair in the middle and combed it much straighter than it used to be. As a matter of fact, at one time he worried that because he looked younger than his age it would jeopardize his application for his residency training in Chicago. He wore casual pants I had never seen him in before.

He asked me, "Did you have trouble traveling in a saree?"

I answered. "No. I am planning to wear a white saree and blouse to work. I will be fine." I was surprised by his question because he seemed to have forgotten that is what we wore in medical school and at the hospitals in India.

Time passed more quickly than we imagined, and suddenly we realized we were the only ones left in the waiting area. We stopped an airline crew member and inquired why they did not call for boarding. We were told that all passengers had boarded, and the aircraft was ready to take off. We had missed the calls while totally engrossed in each other. The doors were closed, and the accordion-ramp had been retracted. We begged him to reopen the door for us to board, but he said his hands were tied.

We needed to get to Chicago, Balu Chettan needed to report to duty at the hospital the next morning, and I too was scheduled to start a new job the next morning as a first year Pathology Resident at West Suburban Hospital in Oak Park, a suburb of Chicago.

Seeing my tears and the despair in our eyes, the crew member was kind enough to encourage an airport officer to telephone into the plane to have the crew reopen the locked door. They phoned the staff to roll the ramp back so we could enter the plane. I am sure the other passengers got a big kick out of a young red-faced couple scrambling to their seats. As soon as we buckled our seat-belts on, the plane rolled off to take its place in line for takeoff to Chicago. We were greatly relieved we hadn't missed the flight, or we would have needed to make excuses for being absent from work the next day. As fate would have it, I did start my Pathology Residency the next day, as scheduled.

# 24

## I Arrive In Chicago

**WHEN THE PLANE** landed in Chicago it was after midnight. Our friends met us at the Chicago O'Hare airport and drove us to our apartment in Berwyn. I knew the street address by heart, because I had addressed umpteen envelopes carrying pages and pages of my love, my tears, and my hopes to my husband for the past seven months.

If first impressions count, I should have turned my tail around and taken the next flight back to where I came from. I was in awe by the countless cars traveling at an immeasurable speed on what appeared to be long ribbons curving into the dark night, which I was told were 'highways.' The oncoming white headlights drew lines passing us on our left while lines of red tail-lights pulsated and changed direction in front of us, very confusing. To my simple question as to how fast we were going, I was told, "Fifty to sixty miles per hour."

Having left my hometown roads just seventy-two hours prior, where the fastest speed a car moved was thirty miles per hour while sharing the road with the slow progress of horse drawn carriages was a contrast to the American highway traffic. Even after midnight, it was unbelievably scary.

Once I arrived in our apartment I unpacked my suitcase and distributed the homeland treasures I had brought for our friends. I had delivered baby pictures of John's firstborn, the baby he had not seen yet. John had come to Chicago in December 1963. Special banana chips from Eipe's mother, which he immediately opened and shared with us. I opened the bag of curry powder, homemade in my mother's kitchen, and invited them for dinner on Sunday. It was 2:30 a.m. on Friday.

As we sat reminiscing, the phone rang. Another friend, Dr. Thomas Bose, called to say he experienced a bad haircut that morning and did not want to shock me in the middle of the night; that is the reason he did not come with the others to meet me at the airport. Since I was to start my residency the next day at the hospital he worked in, he promised to see me there.

I walked around to see what the apartment looked like, since this was to be my home for the next year. There was one spacious room with a large couch against the wall, a window with pale yellow see-thru curtains, open to the darkness of the night, a small dining area holding a wooden table and two chairs leading into a kitchen with a refrigerator, stove, and kitchen sink. When I opened the refrigerator for a can of Pepsi, my back touched the side of the sink. That is how small my kitchen was.

The kitchen in my ammoomma's house had wood-burning stoves which held pots large enough to cook rice for ten to twelve people each meal. The outside sink, where cooking pots were washed was at least three times the size of the kitchen sink I was faced with. This was where I would cook entire meals for the first time in my life. I knew how to make idlis, steamed rice cakes, and I knew how to make my favorite desserts. Knowing I would be 'keeping house' when I came here, I did work with the cook back home to prepare some curries and some vegetable dishes, unique to our part of India. But I had never in my life cooked an entire meal for five people, let alone for the two of us. I took a deep breath and said to myself, "I have to start somewhere. Might as well be here." I sighed.

Returning to the main room, I passed our group of friends and explored on to a dressing area with built-in cabinets and drawers for clothes, and from there into a bathroom.

Where is our bed? Where is our bedroom? I racked my brain and failed to come up with the possibility of a space for the bed. Where has Balu Chettan been sleeping? I did not dare ask him in front of the three other friends. Knowing we had parted as newlyweds just months ago, and knowing this was our first reunion; any mention of a bed would bring an onslaught of ridicule. I was smart enough to hold my tongue. I could barely wait until they left, about 3:30 a.m.

"Where do we sleep?" My question was answered with a burst of laughter, a hug and a kiss.

Balu Chettan took my hand and led me to the couch, pulled out the seat and a full sized bed all made up with fresh white sheets magically appeared. Laughing uncontrollably, he brought out two pillows and a blanket from a cabinet and set out to make the bed.

I burst out crying. My sobs were a release of the tension of departure from my own familiar home combined with the relief that I didn't need to sleep on the floor in my new apartment. I had never seen a hide-away bed before.

1964, Raj and Shaku in the Gables apartment.

# 25

## First Day At Work

**IT WAS COLD.** Very, very, cold.

I thought I came prepared to face a cold Chicago winter. I had brought warm woolen pajama pants, thermal underwear to wear under the lightweight, white nylon sarees. I also wore a warm woolen sweater over my thin cotton choli blouse. It was interesting that a friend of my mother, Nalini Maami, had warned her about how cold the Chicago winter was at the time. She'd experienced a winter in Buffalo, New York when she came to visit her daughter. Hence I was forewarned to bundle up, but it was not enough. Raj had also written to warn me, but the warning signals were not loud enough to alert me prior to my travel preparations. I found out later the cold did not affect him as much as it did me.

When I exited our warm, cozy apartment in Berwyn to travel to the town of Oak Park, where I was to start my first day of work, the bitter cold that assaulted me was nothing I could have expected. I really did not know what to expect. No one can describe how you feel when the harsh unkind winds of winter buffet your body. I thought I would grow used to the weather after living here long enough.

I have learned since then that all new experiences are relative to what we have encountered in the past. Being transplanted from Trivandrum, South India, where it was 110° F in the shade, to Illinois, where in February, it was 10° F in the sun, my body was chilled to its core. I shivered until the car heater kicked in. Soon we reached West Suburban Hospital in Oak Park.

The hospital was taller than any of the hospitals in India with which I was familiar. For that matter, our Medical College and Hospital complex was a sprawling campus that spread out over many miles with separate buildings for the preclinical classes, hospitals to accommodate medical-surgical services, separate buildings for the blood bank, the Women and Childrens Hospitals, and the emergency services. None of those buildings rose over four stories tall.

The drive to the tall building where I was to work was intimidating. Raj parked the car and walked me into the hospital. Two of our friends who worked there, Dr. Radhakrishnan Nair and Dr. Thomas Bose, met me at the front lobby. Both of them were friends who had graduated from the same medical college as Raj and I. Knowing the two friends would take care of me at the new hospital, Raj returned to his hospital in Berwyn and his rotating internship.

The lobby in this hospital was totally different from anything I had seen in India. This hospital welcomed patients with upholstered chairs, glass top tables, handsome hanging lamps and decorative lampshades, which was a far cry from the bare bulbs which hung in many of our hospital corridors back home. Even in the private rooms for our more affluent patients, the chairs were bare backed with minimum cushions to soften the seats.

"Shaku," Radhakrishnan interrupted my observations, "I will take you to the pathology department on the 9th floor. Dr. Kent, Chief of Pathology, is expecting you."

I nodded my head and followed him to the elevators. When we reached the 9th floor, I followed him past the histology laboratory, which I recognized from the smell of formalin and alcohol wafting out through the doors. I saw two curious heads peeking out the large double doors and I was struck by the golden blonde hair atop one. I'd known only an occasional blonde girl among the members of the United States Information Library in Trivandrum, where I spent one

Saturday a month in middle school and high school participating in cultural programs and checking out books.

We walked past another large room with a plaque on the door which declared "Microbiology," and on to the room at the very far end of the corridor. Radhakrishnan knocked on the door, and waited for the "come in," response from within before we entered.

I was introduced to Dr. Geoffrey Kent. Dressed in a tailored dark suit, he looked professorial behind his wooden desk that consumed more than half the floor space. I was drawn to the microscope at the end of a table with the haphazard pile of trays of glass slides containing samples of tissue to be processed for diagnoses. The desk was hidden under heaps of printed paper with handwritten notes while a few books crowded the rest of the desk space. On the wall to my right, two bookshelves were filled with books that brimmed over to the carpeted floor. This was a typical professor's room, and I felt quite at home. I was used to my ammachi's office at the University in Thiruananthapuram where she had a small office at the end of the large Organic Chemistry Research Laboratory. Her office also had piles of paper, but instead of the trays of slides in Dr. Kents' office, there were racks of test tubes on top of one desk and one counter-top, that were always awaiting Ammachi's review.

As Dr. Kent rose from his desk and walked around the table, he grew a good twelve inches taller than I. I had to look up to meet his smiling eyes. His eyes narrowed and his freckled face crinkled around his eyes when he smiled. He reminded me of English gentlemen I had seen in movies back home. I already knew he came from London.

"So you are--," and he purposely drew out the pronunciation of my name, "Dr. Sha-kun-tala Raja-gopal." He shook my hands, taking my right hand in both of his, and kept talking. "You realize I cannot call you by this whole long name. It would take too long. What do your friends call you?"

I was by no means a timid girl by any standards where I came from, but I felt a tad shy and a tad intimidated by his height and his huge hands.

"Shaku," I replied.

"So, Dr. Shaku it will be," he stated in a firm voice.

He led our way out of the room, onto a corridor which led to a few other rooms. Radhakrishnan said goodbye to me. "Page me when you are ready for lunch," he said as he walked back to the elevator.

Passing one or two doors, Dr. Kent turned left into a long narrow room with three desks fastened to each wall with microscopes. At one desk a lovely white lady with soft brown hair, combed and coiffed in a flattering way, sat peering into a microscope. She turned, smiled, and stood to greet me. I guessed she was about thirty. Dr. Kent spoke. "This is Eleanor, our cytologist." Before he introduced me, he turned to look around and asked, "Where is Dr. Bruce?"

"Clara is not here yet," Eleanor replied.

"This is our new resident, Dr. Shaku." Dr. Kent said as he looked from her to me and back. "She says she is a doctor." He leaned toward Eleanor and whispered, but loud enough for me to hear, "I think she is too young to be one. I'm sure she is fibbing." Then he laughed, very pleased with himself at his own joke.

His laugh put me at ease.

Right then we heard the sounds of the elevator door opening not too far from us and the arrival of two people deep in conversation—a woman's voice loud and fast, and the other a man's, speaking softly, slowly, and deliberately—caught my attention.

At the door of the room we were in, they stopped, finished whatever they were discussing, and the woman entered the room. Tall, with a light brown complexion, she looked bossy with a stiff erect stance and an upturned lip that questioned what you were thinking.

"Dr. Clara Bruce, meet Dr. Shakuntala Rajagopal." Dr. Kent introduced us. As we shook hands he continued, "We will call her Dr. Shaku. O.K. Clara?"

With that he turned around and returned to his room.

"So, you are Dr. Rajagopal." Dr. Clara Bruce sat down at the far end of the windowless room, at which I presumed was her desk and microscope.

She pointed toward the desk right behind the one Eleanor was still standing by, and motioned for me to sit down. As soon as I did, Eleanor moved closer to me and said in a very pleasant voice, "We were wondering what we were going to call you. I am relieved you have a short name for us. Your microscope will need adjusting to your small frame."

She turned off her microscope, closed the slide tray she was using, and took my hand in hers. "I am the cytotechnologist here. It is time for my coffee break, so I will take you to the clinical laboratory and blood bank on the fourth floor. Felicia, Lab Manager, has her office there, and you need to get your lab coat, etc. Let's go."

As she unlocked her desk drawer and lifted out her purse, I looked around and took stock of the room that was to be my home away from home for the next four years of my pathology residency. I wondered who else would be using the other tables in our space.

As we walked out of the room, I saw a grey-haired, petite, older lady in a room at the end of the hall. The sign on top of the door said, "Serology." Eleanor took me over to her and said, "Dr. Shaku, this is Sonia. You will be learning a lot from her. She is the best teacher here. Also, she will teach you how to handle Dr. Kent."

I went up to Sonia and shook hands with her. She smiled, and waved away Eleanor's words. "You don't have to worry about Dr. Kent. Just come to me if he gets too strict on you."

I did not know what to say. I just nodded.

We then took the elevator to the fourth floor. I was introduced to two or three people. My head was swimming by that time. I do remember we went to a small office next to the room labelled as blood bank, and met Felicia, Laboratory Manager. She thanked Eleanor for bringing me to her, and asked her a further favor–to take me to the coat room.

In the coat room, I had to spell out my name to the seamstress who was to give me two white coats of proper size with my name embroidered above the left top pocket. I was to pick them up later that day. Then we went to the second floor to the cafeteria for a coffee break. I was surprised I did not need to pay for my food. The interns and residents were not paid much, I was to make $400 a month, but we received three free meals per day.

Later I met the two other pathologists on the staff, and the members of the histology department where the tissue samples from surgery were processed and slides were made for me to read. As a resident I had to make my diagnosis and then the pathologist in charge each day reviewed and signed out the cases.

It was a good thing I did not know about jet lag. Maybe I was too young and naïve to think beyond life as anything other than the open book before me, where at that point in time I was meant to learn and absorb all I needed in order to become an excellent pathologist.

Looking back, the mentors, even the bossy ones, the fellow struggling residents, the dedicated technologists, the lovely ladies in the kitchen and the wise physician friends on the staff at that hospital, all helped form my character and confidence that has sustained me all these years. This was not only my place of work, it was also my first adopted family home, where I spent more of my waking hours than at my real home each week for the next few years.

1964. The pathology resident's room.
My home away from home for five and a half years.

# 26

## Westward Ho

**TWO WEEKS AFTER** I arrived in the U.S.A. my dear Raj announced to me, "We are going on vacation to California in May."

It took me by surprise. "How can we do that? I have just started my residency at West Suburban. I can't ask for a vacation so soon!"

"You don't have to. I already procured you the days off from Dr. Kent."

I was totally perplexed. Raj sat there with a naughty grin on his face enjoying every second of my confusion.

Raj had arranged for a two week vacation for us to California and back, driving all the way with three friends (Radahakrishnan, Eipe, and Rajasekharan),because their first year stint was ending in June, and all four of them were eligible for their annual days off. However, I just started my first year training in February and was not eligible for my annual vacation. Yet, I found out that Dr. Kent, my boss, had already approved it. My theory is he felt sorry for the pining look in Raj's eyes when he explained the request for my early vacation even before I started my new job. Anyway, he did grant my days off to co-incide with theirs, and we planned to drive cross country to explore the 'West.'

Since we only had visa permits to stay for five years, until the end of our residency training, we wished to see as much of the country as possible. What better way to do that than driving all the way west to the Pacific coast?

Mrs. Florence Hrusa was the medical staff secretary at MacNeal Memorial Hospital where Raj worked; she acted like a mother hen to all the young naïve interns who came to her door with problems. She took me into her fold and called me the week after I arrived to tell me that I could ask for her help anytime I needed it. She was a tall, beautiful lady with a well cut coif of silver hair, a pleasant smile and a soft kind voice, she was approachable to even somewhat shy interns like Raj. Raj consulted with Mrs. Hrusa to help put an itinerary together for our trip in May.

I included photos of our itinerary to show how crazy and ambitious this idea was, but of course we did not see it that way.

| | Place | Dep. Time | Miles | Driving Time | Arrival | Place | Plans |
|---|---|---|---|---|---|---|---|
| 8th | Los Angeles | 7 PM | 227 | 5.30 | 12.30 mid | Paso Robles | Moving Land Way Marineland > STAY |
| 9th | Paso Robles | 10 AM | 201 | 4.00 | 2 PM | San Francisco | Muir Woods. Bridges. STAY |
| 10th | San Francisco | 1 PM | 93 | 2.00 | 3 PM | Sacramento | Boat Ride Train Ride Rose Garden |
| | Sacramento | 4 PM | 140 | 3.00 | 7 PM | Reno | |
| | Reno | 9 PM | 167 | 3.00 | 12 MN | Winnemucka | STAY |
| 11th | Winnemucka | 10 AM | 176 | 3.30 | 1.30 PM | Wells | Lunch |
| | Wells | 3 PM | 186 | 3.30 | 6.30 PM | Salt Lake City | Dinner Sight seeing Mormon Temple |
| | Salt Lake City | 8 PM | 300 | — | — | — | > Yellowstone National Park |
| 12th | | | Yellowstone 117 | National Park. Codi | | | STAY |
| 13th | Codi | 10 AM | 154 108 156 | | | Murdo > | Mt. Rushmore. Rapid City. STAY. |

| | Place | Departure | Miles | Driving Time | Arrival-Place | |
|---|---|---|---|---|---|---|
| 14th | Murdo | 10 Am | 542. | — | Nite La Crosse | STAY. |
| 15th | La Crosse | 10 Am | 90 | — | Wisconsin Dells | |
| | | | 70 | | Madison | |
| | | | 150 | | Chicago. | > Home. - STAY. Have Fun. |

Good Luck. + have a nice trip.

The plan was to drive Rt. 66 for the most part, see the country first hand, and once we got to California, drive from Los Angeles to San Francisco, before heading back.

We were all very excited and talked about the places we wished to see. Radhakrishnan really wanted to spend an extra night in Las

Vegas, so the unanimous decision was to drive through the first and third night in order to get to Las Vegas earlier. Since I did not know how to drive a car, I was designated to sleep in the afternoons when there was a long strip of highway driving, and stay up with the night-driver to keep him company so he did not fall asleep.

By the end of March I found out I was pregnant. Between rejoicing about our good news and anticipating our road trip, Raj expressed his concern regarding our pregnancy, and considered canceling the trip. Raj was quite upset, and of course we did not want to cancel the trip. We did not want to miss the opportunity to see the country in the company of dear responsible friends. One more concern was how I had morning sickness that lasted well into afternoons, and some evenings too. This posed a problem. After lengthy discussion among the two of us and then with our three co-travelers-to-be, it was decided as long as I was healthy, there was no need to cancel the vacation.

The case of my morning sickness was also solved. Doctors Radhakrishnan and Eipe gathered half a dozen IV sets and nutrient bottles to carry with us so I could be fed intravenously if we ran into a major health problem with my 'throwing up' along the way.

We set out in the middle of May, following Route 66. Our first stop was Springfield, Illinois, where we visited President Abraham Lincoln's home. I did not have too much problem with my nausea. At our lunch stop, I ordered hot soup. The saltine crackers and the salty soup kept my stomach from acting up. Dinner was just toast and jelly because I could not stand the smell of cheese in a sandwich nor could I taste of the bland chicken or fish. We also decided that at every meal one of us would order soup. The saltines in the basket were immediately saved in the guys' pockets to tide over my hunger between meals.

Meramec Caverns in Missouri was a marvel to behold. *'Air conditioned by Mother Nature,'* as the marquee proclaimed. Radhakrishnan wished to spend at least two nights in the casino in Las Vegas. In order to have enough time and a little extra money to spend there, we had decided to drive through the night. We made it to Las Vegas with plenty of time to spend and money we could spare. We reached the town at dusk, and as we drove through the Strip, the night lights came on. I said in awe, "Wonder how many light bulbs are used on this street alone. They must be using more electricity to light up this street than is used for the entire Trivandrum town."

All four of them had a great laugh at my expense. I have not heard the end of that quote of mine in all the years that followed.

Las Vegas fascinated me for many other reasons too. I loved the slot machines immediately. I knew I had to come back there in the future when I could afford more than the penny slots.

We sat in the crowd of a small venue, having dinner and watching Totie Fields. She was heavy and had a very friendly, yet risqué dialogue. I wore a saree and long ear rings. I must have caught her attention.

"Hey, you young thing from India over there!" She bellowed in my direction. I just smiled. "How much do you weigh?" She continued with a wicked laugh. "Placing her palm under her left breast she went on. "Half as much as my one side?" and raised her breast lightly with a naughty wink. The crowd clapped and I covered my face with my hands. "Don't be shy," she said, waved at our table, and went on with the show.

We continued to enjoy the rest of the strip and other shows for the next day.

The four men, acting more like boys, took turns sleeping during the day, and I too slept when I could. I did not know how to drive a car. So, it was my turn to keep the night-driver company. I did so by talking, singing songs, and telling stories about our parents and siblings.

In New Mexico, hedge-rows of oleanders touted masses of pink and white flowers and Balu Chettan had me posing for pictures beside them. I still remember the pink floral design in the cotton saree I wore when I posed in front of the oleanders.

*I closed my eyes and was carried back to my ammoomma's front yard. There, the aralis, as we called the oleanders, welcomed the caterpillars that metamorphosed into shiny dumbbell-shaped cocoons which hung precariously from the tip of their dark, long leaves. As kids we were allowed to pick some and place them in a shoe box with holes in the lid. We waited impatiently until they released the butterflies in due time. The arali leaves were poisonous to their predators, but not to the caterpillars that feasted on them before their metamorphosis turned into the cocoon stage, and energy for the transformation to the butterfly stage. It taught me early in life that some things that are good for someone else may not be good for me, and vice versa.*

*It was fascinating to stop and visit an Indian plantation. I pumped water from a bore-well and we drank the cold, fresh water that gushed out. Little children with light and dark brown skin like us ran up to look at our brown skin color. Both groups were 'Indians,' yet their facial features, especially the cheek structure, was distinctly different. It struck me that the chatter and the smiles were just the same. I don't know who was inspecting the other group more intently.*

Disneyland, the Magic Kingdom that Walt Disney had conjured up and built blew my mind away. The rides were beyond anything I had imagined. The Jungle cruise took us through rain forests and, turning a curve in the river, I came face to face with a large Ganesha statue with a waterfall bathing him. Involuntarily, *"Ganesha Sharanam...."* a prayer seeking refuge in Lord Ganesha, came to my lips. We rode past an Indian camp with wigwams and Native Indians around a campfire spewing darts of fire and smoke, complete with the Indians' loud singing and even louder drums. For a few moments we were in a land we had never been before. Soon the course of the river took us through wilderness where a pack of elephants were bathing in the water. One even trumpeted and sprayed water toward the boat we were in.

The Matterhorn Mountain attracted us and we took a ride up the mountain in bob-sleds. It was a rickety ride. But what we did not know was it was also a roller-coaster ride. I screamed every time we dropped down a slope. I was relieved when the ride ended. I could not believe we were so naïve that we went on the ride without knowing what it entailed. And me, three months pregnant! Oh, well. We were only in our early twenties, and not very world-wise, yet. And we were ambitious.

Many years later I had the good fortune to visit the same mountain with our three daughters, and I did not ride the bob-sleds. But, in 2016 when my sixteen-year-old grandson, Travis, asked me to ride it with him, I did. I did not feel scared even though I knew what to expect. I did scream each time we dipped down within a cave or a slope and took a deep breath of relief when the ride ended. The make believe moments in life are truly exciting. As I write this I think of the song from the movie *"Paper Moon." It wouldn't be make believe, If I believed in you..."*

We went to the Hollywood Wax Museum. Life-size wax figures of Elvis, Marilyn Monroe, Bette Davis and many other famous figures took us back in history. The entire trip in Los Angeles was magical and many times I wished Shanthi my sister was with me. Many years later I was fortunate to share the magic with Shanthi at a different Disney place in Florida, at Disney World.

Knott's Berry farm had gastronomical delights such as orange marmalade with English muffins they served at the restaurant. For the first time in my life I tasted apple butter. I still look forward to places that serve apple butter.

By now my head was spinning. What with the lack of sleep and all the fantasy and fun thrown at me in such a short time, I am surprised I was still ready to go on to San Francisco and beyond as we planned.

The trip along the Pacific coast to San Francisco was along Rt.1, and we made good time getting to northern California. The wineries and the stately mansions we passed delighted me. Of course, we had to stop for wine-tasting at a real winery. I was not drinking any alcoholic beverages. I stuck to grape juice.

Fishermen's Wharf is an unforgettable experience for the variety of foods and the crowds in the small space. I could not eat much with all the fried fish smells combined with the various cheeses. I survived on bread and butter and soup. I could not stand the smell of the chowder, but years later I came to like it a lot.

I cannot state and restate enough how ambitious we were. From San Francisco we crossed over the Rockies to Utah to listen to the Mormon Tabernacle Choir. Anything different from what we grew up with... we had to see. We were all planning to return to our hometowns after our training and did not want to miss anything.

*Through marriages and childbirths, and despite some dry years, and despite illnesses, divorce, and retirements, and a bit of moving around the country, this band of travelers along with most of our families have stayed in touch. Those two weeks on the road created a bond for the few of us whose hearts were pining for our own siblings we had left behind.*

1964, Raj& Shaku, San Francisco

With Mickey in Disneyland

# 27

## Learning To Survive

ONE OF THE hardest things I encountered in Chicago during February 1964, was my first cold winter in the USA. I could not just open a door and walk outside to the street and catch a bus like I did back home. I could not go to the grocery store to buy food, or walk to the temple to put flowers in front of Lord Ganesha, or by the feet of Goddess Parvathi. Those were routines that kept me grounded and my life on track in my past life in Trivandrum, and I missed them.

Since I did not know how to drive a car, I depended on a colleague to give me rides to and from work. At 7:00 a.m., Monday through Friday, I met Ms. Eleanor Goldberg, in front of the McNeal Memorial Hospital in Berwyn. She was the cytotechnologist in our pathology department. At the end of each day she drove me back to the same place. This meeting place was only two blocks from my apartment building where Raj and I lived, but the one-to-two foot tall snowdrifts made the sidewalks treacherous and my morning trek laborious. For this tropical bird, it might as well been the Himalayan mountains... it was a rough walk in the beginning.

I felt restricted and snowbound. It was strange how I could not step out and meet my friends as I did when I went to college, or catch a bus to go play tennis. It took me over a half hour to bundle up in sweaters and coats and tie up laced boots, before I walked out of our apartment. Our car was parked in the street. Before we could drive anywhere we had to warm up the car. It took us at least fifteen minutes to remove the snow and ice from the windows. Even for the short walk down the street to buy groceries I had to bundle in layers for my walk in the snow.

I could not walk to a temple to pray. I could not be driven to a temple either, since there were no Hindu temples in the Chicagoland area. So, it was really a moot point.

I knew in my heart and mind that God is everywhere, and God can hear our prayers from our Pooja room at home as well as he/she could from the temple Sanctum, but it did not feel the same. The comfort I drew from the ritual of taking a bath, donning clean clothes, walking to the temple, offering flowers to Ganesha and to Parvathi Devi were all missing. The rituals gave me a feeling of surrender. Surrendering all my actions, cares, and hopes to the almighty God gave me a feeling of an invisible, yet powerful support, like a wind beneath my wings to soar as high as I wanted to in life.

I missed that feeling. I realized I needed to retrain my mind and heart to depend on myself to get things done. Also the God-power needed to come from within me, and not the idols who I had been trained to look up to for support until that time in my life.

Although the restrictions bothered me initially, the realization that I was finally reunited with the love of my life, and the fact that every morning I woke up beside him, did cheer me up.

We wrote to my parents, my ammachi and my ammoomma, and Thankom Maami regularly.

Once a week we received mail from Maami and Ammachi. My mother wrote once in a while. I looked forward to the letters from home. It was very seldom that we called. In the first place we had to book a trunk-call and have the operator call us back when the connection was obtained. My ammoomma did not have a phone in the Chenthitta House,so I longed to hear her voice and Ammachi's voice. I called my father and mother, and my sister-in-law, Ambika, but as soon as the first three minutes were used, it was time to hang up because

there were additional charges after that. The time restriction bothered me, I had so much to say, and so many questions for them, and
the short conversations were never long enough. I was too young to
be thankful that at least I had those moments.

The good thing was our thoughts were focused on patients when
Raj and I worked Monday through Saturday, and some Sundays.
Otherwise, we might be obsessed thinking about our families back in
India.

I did not comprehend how deep the trauma of my separation from
all my loved ones affected my daily life. In the glow of my husband's
love I managed well to mask the sorrow of being torn from the comfort and warmth of my family back home. Until one day, when trying
to buy the par-boiled rice that I was accustomed to, I realized we could
not afford It. It was much more expensive than the regular long grain
rice. I had nobody to complain to. I could not cry at the store. After I
returned to our apartment, I went to the bathroom, and bathed away
my sorrows, I cried in the shower until I depleted my tears. It opened
my eyes to the fact that there was no genie in the form of Ammachi
or my daddy to make all my wishes come true anymore. I needed to
grow up.

Growing up was not as hard as I thought after my first shock of
realization. All I needed to do was buckle up, hop on the horse, and
ride forward. My first venture was to find spices for my Indian curries
and other dishes. Red pepper powder in 3oz bottles would only last
for a week or so. The cinnamon powder in the same quantities may
last for a month or six weeks. At our salaries of $400 a month, my
Indian cuisine would be cost-prohibitive. I spoke to Sasi, who was my
new friend from India down the hall, and she gave me the address of
a store in New York where I could purchase my spices in bulk, 1/2lb. or
1lb. packages at much more reasonable costs. All I had to do was mark
the appropriate box on an order sheet which Sasi gave me, and send
a money order with shipping costs included. A week later the spices
would come in the mail. Now my problem was to get to the bank before it closed to procure the money order. I had to wait till Friday when

the bank was open till 8:00 p.m. because I came home at 6:00p.m. and the bank closed at 5:00 p.m. the rest of the week. It was frustrating, but I managed.

I thought of all the things I took for granted. My ammachi or my mother would make a list of all the spices and accouterments and the errand boy would drop it off at the provisions store at the beginning of the month. A day later the manager or his assistant brought cardboard boxes filled with the packets and gave Ammachi the bill for the previous month. Ammachi usually paid cash for that bill. The bill for the current month came later, the next month. The lady who worked in the kitchen checked the packages against the list and reported to Ammachi if everything was in order. Very seldom did I hear of any discrepancies.

The vegetables were brought to the door by vendors, usually ladies who carried them in round baskets on their heads. We bought only the items needed for cooking in one or two days. We did not have a refrigerator to store them for longer periods. It was not a problem because the lady came back in two days with more.

I could not believe my eyes when I walked into the grocery store called National, two blocks from home. Mounds of all sorts of vegetables and fruits made my eyes bulge. I could not decide which ones to buy first. Shiny green skin of the cucumbers, glossy eggplants, and even the shiny skin of the apples made them look like wax figurines. Sasi told me they were really waxed. Especially the apples. Aisles filled with packaged cereals made it very difficult to choose. Packages of rice, long grain, par-boiled, instant rice, all in varied sizes. I had only seen rice in large gunny sacks, or stored in large wooden containers. I had no idea how long the small plastic bags of rice would last. One thing was sure. I was buying the long grain rice. The par-boiled rice was too expensive, indeed.

The packets of candy and the chocolates were very tempting. But it was the meat aisle that fascinated me. I had no idea which one to buy. Rows and rows of beef with eight different labels, lamb chops and shoulder meat, and beef roast and lamb roast. And the different cuts of pork, all made my head spin. I stuck to chicken since I did not eat pork or beef. Even the chicken packages were confusing. Breasts were in different packs. But cut up whole chicken was cheaper. So I bought that. Only problem was, once I got it home I had to discard the neck, and the layer of fat covering the thighs and breasts. That was not acceptable. I had never cut up chicken into smaller chunks for curry before, this was my first time. All of the preparations to cook seemed laborious. Raj and his friend, Rajasekharan, had done some cooking in the seven months before I came, but Rajasekharan was the one who cooked the chicken. Raj was of no help in solving my problem. Soon I learned that buying skinless breast pieces and thighs without all the other distractions was more economical and practical.

Each day was a learning experience. At McDonald's Raj ordered cheeseburgers. I could not bring myself to eat beef. I ate French fries and drank Coke. At a pizza place not too far from our Gables building everyone raved about pizza. The cheese smell did not sit well with me. I would rather break my religious code and eat beef to survive than eat the cheese on the pizza. We picked up a hamburger for me and went to the pizzeria. While Raj and friends ate pizza - I ate my hamburger. I brought my chopped lemon pickle from India with me, and put some pieces of lemon and the red pepper sauce in between the buns to spice up the hamburger. I changed when I needed to. To survive. To flourish in this land where fate landed me, I was not going to starve and wither away.

And then, five months later my bosom buddy, Padma, and her husband arrived from Trivandrum bearing more spices and special snack goods. They moved into the apartment across the hall in the Gables building where we lived. We spent all of our time together except when we went to work. They were newly married and like us all their experiences replicated what I had gone through, and Raj before me. We decided to shop, cook and live together as one family. Paapa (Padma) did not start working right away because she still had to take the ECFMG qualifying exams. She did the cooking during the day and I contributed at night after I returned from work. On weekends it was the same routine. I worked every Saturday and many Sundays. When all four of us were home we watched television. Being this was our first exposure to television viewing, and with so many shows to choose from, it was quite an exciting experience. It was easy to get caught up in the drama of serials and the movies were very tempting. In 1964 most programs were in black and white, some were in color. At the end of 1964 NBC moved to all color television and adopted the multicolor peacock as the company symbol. If it wasn't for some of the discipline we exercised, our scientific reading for our residency training and the studies for our exams would have suffered immensely. We continued to watch the evening news and the nightly news; they were still very important to us.

All four of us attended the same Medical College. Paapa and I were classmates since after high school. The same with Raj and Paapa's husband, Shanmugha Sundaram. I had known Shanmugham because my ammoomma was his family doctor. She took care of his diabetic grandmother, and helped his mother deliver many of his siblings. Also, all of our parents knew each other.

At the time when my homesickness peaked and lowered my mood, Paapa's arrival helped tide over some of the issues.

Also, the spices from home were replenished; this helped my mindset while transitioning into a new culture with so little Indian ethnicity. A few months later I sent another order for spices to New York. A week later the order was returned without the spices. The letter stated the shipping charges had increased and my money order was short by 43 cents. Hence I had to place a new order with the proper amount. I cried. This meant I needed to run around after work hours, get home in time to change the money order at the bank and mail it to New York. The postage was only six cents for mailing the letter. It was the additional delay in receiving my spice-supply which upset me the most. At my earliest opportunity I re-sent the order to New York. I did not have a choice. I had managed the situation. Yet, I felt sorry for myself and moped around for a couple of days. One evening after I said my prayers I shook off my dejection, and said to myself how dejection would only bring sadness to my heart. So, I decided to break out of it, determined to make the best of the land where fate had landed me. I decided to educate myself about the people, the culture and the foods. I felt a heavy load taken off my head as soon as I accepted my goal of savoring and enjoying what America offered me at the moment.

I learned I had to embrace the darkness of my helpless moments and draw from my light within to reveal the way to move forward in my life.

# 28

## The Things I Carried

**THE THINGS** I carried when I came to this country were dictated partly by the rituals of my Hindu heritage. In my luggage I had a solid silver oil lamp, about eight inches tall, that took five wicks and had the capacity to hold one ounce of oil, enough to burn a single wick for about one hour. My Hindu custom required that the prayers be offered in front of an oil lamp. But, once I started my residency in pathology, the daily routine of prayers lasted less than fifteen minutes at the lamp because that was all I could spare in any twenty-four hours.

I was twenty-three years old when I came to the States from South India, and I tried to be pragmatic about things I brought with me. But sentiment overruled pragmatism on more than one item that was included in my luggage. A brown leather suitcase was chosen instead of a *metal trunk* to make the most of the weight restrictions of what I could carry.

I carried with me a jar of coconut oil, boiled and cooled with black peppercorns, to maintain the gloss in my hair. Ammachi made me promise that I would prepare more of it when that jar was empty. One of my most cherished childhood memories was of *oil bath* Sundays. We ran and played in our courtyard, shiny and half-naked, with warm oil rubbed lovingly all over our bodies by our mother or aunt. The smell of the black peppers in that oil is still with me. And I can feel the tenderness of their palms on my skin.

I brought a unique steaming pot to make *Idlis. Idlis* are steamed rice cakes. The batter required takes over one hour to grind the *urad* lentil and rice grain (at the ratio of 1:3) twenty-four hours to let the batter rise, and twenty minutes to cook. The pot has two special trays atop a water section, and a domed lid to trap the steam. Once cooked it takes barely one minute to down an idli. Smothered with butter and sugar, they are so devilishly delightful. Idlis are breakfast food where I come from. With little time for sit-down breakfasts, I made them for supper on Monday nights. Only vegetarian fare was served at my table on Mondays, the day of my *Shiva Vratham,* a fast in honor of Lord Shiva, for the health and happiness of my husband. If the head of the household stayed healthy and happy, the rest of the family would be happy too.

Also included was a *chattukam,* a metal spatula, the thinnest ever, to turn over *dosas.* These were pancakes made without eggs or leavening, and ones that would stick to the griddle unless extra care was taken in handling them. Just as with some people, they will crack if not handled with care.

In addition to the white saris and blouses to be worn at the hospital, I packed a dozen *baadis,* special bras that I wore. A baadi is a short chemise tied up in a knot in front, thus flattening one's figure and masking any curves, an effort at modesty, in those times. I thought it quite contradictory that while we took pride in the feminine spirit, and in having sensuous bodies, adorned them in gold and silver, there existed traditional efforts at covering up and hiding aspects of sexuality. To play tennis, I had to wear *salwar-kammeez* outfits, long pajama-pants worn with long loose-fitting shirts, and a shawl draped across the chest, because Ammoomma did not allow me to wear tennis shorts. Wasted efforts at modesty, as I look back. But then my ammoomma's word was dictum, and I obeyed. Yet my ammoomma allowed short choli blouses with our saris that left our mid-riff bare. Not that I complained.

The *baadis* were eventually replaced by regular bras when I had to go to the hospital here in the States for the delivery of my first-born. It was too embarrassing for my husband that in 1964 I still wore undergarments from the stone ages.

The baggage of superstitions I bore would stifle an army. While many were self-assuring, others, if I allowed them to, could have destroyed me.

I carried the firm belief that touching my husband's feet in respect first thing in the morning was equivalent to honoring God, for he is the first image of God that I saw when I woke up. I did that, and felt blessed that I had a loved one that I could so honor.

The sense of optimism imbued within me assured that as an agent of God, I could do what is right and honorable even in dishonorable situations. I held a conviction that while one should compromise in times of conflicts, one need not jeopardize one's principles. As wise as I was for a twenty-three-year-old, the conflicts remained, and as the Western life molded me, many such beliefs came in handy for survival.

I came with the confidence that I could do good for many people, and I did. When my efforts were fruitful, I thanked God. When my efforts did not work out, I laid them at God's feet and accepted failure, praying for strength to bear the disappointment.

In my bag was a dog-eared cookbook in *Malayalam*, my native language. It belonged to Ammachi. She had depended on the book for her culinary efforts, which were at best sporadic and not highly regarded even by herself, but what little she did was based on this little cookbook which was authentic South Indian, Kerala cooking. Unadulterated by any north Indian recipes, she felt I needed it. It was her ultimate sacrifice for my future. I guard it from wind, rain, oil splatters and fire, and will pass it on to the next generations, even though they cannot read it.

In my brown leather suitcase I also carried an ivory figure of Lord Krishna. It had to be very old. My mother's uncle carried it with him to Burma during World War II, and when he returned, it was placed on a shelf in his drugstore--the one my ammoomma, his sister, bought for him. It was the corner drugstore by my house and across the street from the Government Hospital for Women and Children. I hung out there as a youngster. When I was old enough, he let me wash the mortars and pestles after he used them. At dusk, our time of daily prayers, I was allowed to light an oil lamp in front of this ivory Krishna. By all standards the store should have prospered. But for reasons unknown to me, the store closed when I was about eleven or twelve. When he packed up his things, I stood there sadly, not knowing what to say. As he took the statue off the shelf, he handed it to me. Standing three inches tall, the smiling face of Krishna seemed to say 'take me.' I took it with me to my medical college hostel, and I included it in the things I carried when I came over here. My great uncle has since passed away.

And then there was this pink purse in a floral design with sparkling thread woven on the top. It was a birthday gift from my husband Raj, three years before we got married. It was a turbulent time in our lives, with his father opposing our relationship, and placing undue pressure on Raj while he was struggling to keep up with his studies in Medical School. That year, on my birthday, Raj decided that he was not going to celebrate it with me. His closest friend and confidante, T.K. Rajan, thought that he was wrong. So, Rajan himself went to town, bought a purse for Raj to gift me, and arranged for us to meet at *The Canteen*, the café on Campus, our usual hangout. Rajan then coerced Raj to give me my birthday present. How could I not bring that with me to Chicago, as I traveled 10,000 miles away from home?

I had a reel-tape of Malayalam songs made for us to listen to in our new abode, so far away. On the day we recorded the songs, my daddy said a few words of greeting to my husband who was already in the States. Thus I would have my daddy's voice with me forever. My dad would pass away seven years later. I could not have known then that I would never see my dad again, or how I would wish I had more of his voice to listen to.

Also included was a necklace and two bangles made of 22 karat gold with ruby red finial stones set in an unique design, that my am-moomma gave as part of my wedding jewelry. The rest of my jewelry had to be left behind, because I was traveling alone, and because we were planning to return after four years of residency training. Back then, there was no intention of staying here forever.

My album of photographs included pictures of my daddy and mummy before they gave up three piece suits and gold lace saris for clothes sewn from the khadi cloth. In my oldest memories, I see them wearing clothes made of the rough khadi cloth that was handwoven cotton, made in India with pride. It symbolized the principle touted by Mahatma Gandhi, *the Father of our Nation,* who as part of the anti- British protest, shunned all items bearing any Western influence. Khadi-making was one small industry established by the Gandhian movement, enabling the peasant folk to make a living with a sense of pride.

There are pictures of me in this album at six months, butt naked lying on my tummy wearing only a toothless smile. There is a similar baby picture of my future husband as well. A series of pictures graced the pages. These were taken at my husband's home, long before we got married, when we were still in our teens, alongside our siblings. As family friends, we had periodic get-togethers, and my dad, being a photographer, imprinted many of these gatherings in celluloid.

Also included were photographs of my childhood chums while we participated in various musical and drama functions in junior college and medical college. There were wedding portraits of my sister Shanthi at age fifteen, and my ammachi at twenty-eight. This album is one of the most precious possessions I brought with me. The photos were to remind me of my family experiences, and of how to make a difference in the world. Many were symbolic of Ammoomma's blessed advice, "Remember all what I have taught you. Even as you reach for the skies, keep your feet solidly on the ground." I smile as I peruse them, even now.

In 1951, when I was eleven years old, I had the good fortune of taking a tour of North India with my ammoomma. Traveling from my subtropical home in Kerala where temperatures ranged from 80 to 110 degrees, to Delhi and Agra at 50 degrees in January, I wore woolen pants under my cotton skirts. Since the weather in Chicago would be colder by comparison, my mother made me pack the woolen pants. Thermal underwear of sorts, I found them handy in adapting from the sweltering heat of 110 degrees in the shade to the freezing cold of 10 degrees in the sun. The woolen pants were of a loose drawstring pattern. So it fit me even though eleven years had passed after I first used them.

My husband came to Chicago in June, 1963, and I followed him seven months later. While I pined for him in the interim, I drove my family crazy. My mother suggested that I knit a sweater for my husband. So I did. I used gray wool in a *cable and purl* pattern. I made a scarf to match. He said he loved it, and wore it a few times. But once we could afford smoother, less patterned sweaters, it was placed in the back of the closet. It served its purpose when I needed an activity to keep me sane.

In Trivandrum, there is an Ashram where Dad and Mom went regularly for worship and group prayers and all the children accompanied them whenever possible. The *Guruji,* respected teacher, Swami Abhedananda had given my mother a copy of *The Bhagavat Geetha,* to follow along when she attended discourses about the philosophy of life and death and the wisdom of living.

My mother graciously donated me her personal copy of *The Bhagavat Geetha,* the book that is considered the *Bible* for us Hindus. The big difference is that the Geetha is more of a road map for living the Hindu life than a book of rules to live by. The Geetha sums up the words of wisdom Lord Krishna imparted to the young Prince Arjuna when Arjuna broke down on the battlefield of Kulashetra. The battle was between good and evil--principles followed and fairness in life sustained, between the two sets of cousins, the Pandavas and the Kauravas in the Epic of Mahbharata. The words of divine wisdom in the Bhagavat Geetha are the most relevant words ever spoken to guide us in living a Hindu life. Hence the act of giving up her book for my future was a very unselfish act on my mother's part. She did not have a selfish bone in her body.

The things I carried then served their purpose in my life transition to this land. They anchor me in times of turbulence. They remind me of all the love that came with them and still guide me to transcend my own issues and help my family by the stories of the strong women and men who shaped my character. My relationship to them still contributes to my sanity and survival.

# 29

## A Child Is Born

As I said, in March I found out I was with child.

Raj and I were elated.

I grew up as the oldest child in our house with the privileged status of being the 'first granddaughter' of Dr. Chellamma and the 'first daughter' of the famous Photographer Sivaraam.

Raj was the oldest of ten children, and the first-born son who was denied nothing until he coveted me against his father's wishes, when we were both medical students. The untimely demise of his father, the year Raj graduated from medical school, had changed everything between him and his mother. His status as her favorite son was re-established in his mother's eyes. He was her sole source of financial support. He assumed the role as head of the household, one that carried nine siblings of whom only one was married and on her own.

So, here we were, bringing forth a child who would inherit all the crown and glory of a worthy descendant of two firstborns.

The two of us laughed and cried while we celebrated the event.

We could not go out to eat, because there were no restaurants that catered to my cravings. No chicken curry, no fried fish marinated in a paste of ground onions, coriander, ginger, red pepper, black pepper and salt. I craved the spicy Kerala chicken curry, smothered in red pepper, and lots of it, sour, dark tamarind and other hot spices. When it comes to fish curry, if it did not make my eyes water, it was not spicy enough for my taste. We could not afford to eat at any restaurant other than McDonalds. McDonald's golden arches touted "first billion burgers sold,' that year. We could not hide our happy news from any of our friends; we were glowing all the time, and I was throwing up every time I smelled meat cooking.

There was no immediate family here in America with whom to celebrate. Instead our dear friends gathered as extended family to celebrate our joy. When I cooked a meal, each of the guys who had never washed a plate or a cup before in India, gladly scrubbed my pots and pans, cleared my table, and even put away my place mats. Then we sat and talked about our childhood back home and how their mothers reacted to their pregnancies.

Raj and I sang the songs about firstborns and newborns we had learned from Malayalam movies.

*'Adyathe kanamani aanayirikkenan, avan achane pole irikkenunum'*
*The first born has to be a boy, and he has to look like his father.*
We sang…

*"adyathe kanmani pennayirikkenum, aarume kandal kothikkananum; aval ammaye pole chirikkanam"*
*The first born has to be a girl, and anyone who sees her has to covet her; she should smile like her mother."*

We sang the songs, we laughed, and then I burst into tears. "I want my Mommy," I would say between sobs.

I missed my mother the most, now that I was being blessed with child, I wondered what I could do? It was too far for me to travel. We had too many commitments to just quit and leave, and besides, we just plain could not afford to return home even for a visit.

My sleep patterns were all goofed up and dreams interrupted my sleep.

I still remember the time when I woke up in the middle of the night, and screamed, "I want to see Kannan, now!"

*Kannan* was our nephew, and the littlest member of our family we had left behind. The year after I married Raj, Kannan's mother, Ambika, had another baby, so to help Ambika I took care of baby Kannan many times.

Carrying my child brought the homesickness and the yearning for my own mother, and the one child, my nephew, to whom I had been close. The fact that no one here would pamper me the way mothers-to-be were pampered back home hit me hard. A mother-to-be would get her favorite foods brought to her not only by her mother and mother-in-law, but also by her aunts and close family friends. Even my dad would have stopped by Xavier's Restaurant in town for my favorite vanilla ice cream. A pregnant woman was also treated to an oil massage with warm herbal oils by the ladies working in the kitchen at least once a week before lunch, and bathed with warm water, and towel dried gently. After lunch a mandatory afternoon nap followed. I did not want such physical pampering, but I missed all the fuss by the moms and the rest of the family that I would have enjoyed if I was in Thiruananthapuram.

My emotional state made an impact on Raj. The next evening he offered to buy me tickets to return home for a short visit. I did not accept his offer.

Even though I was in a tizzy due to my 'hormonal' ups and downs, I knew my returning alone even for a visit was not a simple affair. I think Raj's offer to give me a visit home was all I needed to hear, because I settled down and went about my business without too many more outbursts like that one.

Thinking back, Raj was not much older than me, he was only twenty-five years old at the time. I see now how Raj handled his emotions and mine very well, and acted quite wise. In retrospect, I am still impressed by his reaction.

I was eleven years old when my mother was pregnant with her fifth child. At the same time my aunt was carrying her first child. As was the custom in our society, close family members brought my aunt her favorite foods. More of the snack and dessert kind than real food.

When she was six months pregnant the family held a special celebration called 'vyakku-koda.' Of course the celebration was centered around food, different kinds of food, sweet, salty and spicy food items.

An oil lamp was lit, trays of fruits and flowers placed in front of the lamp and incense sticks burning spread an aroma of calm among the noisy family crowd who had gathered. Trays filled with different sweetmeats to represent the sixth month of pregnancy were placed by the lamp. My aunt, decked in our traditional *mundu* and *neriyathu* outfit was escorted ceremoniously to a low wooden seat placed to the side of the lamp and accouterments. The *mundu* is a wrap made of cotton material and her mundu had a shiny border of gold-dipped threads. The neriyathu is like the top half of a saree, and was wrapped around her, the last yard draped over her left shoulder. As I remember, she wore a gold-colored blouse and her wedding jewelry. She glowed in her pregnancy and her happiness. Her parents, her sisters and families all joined us in my ammoomma's home to celebrate.

One by one the ladies in the family took pieces of her favorite foods, and wishing her a safe pregnancy and delivery, placed them in her mouth piece by piece. Everyone clapped and the room filled with laughter that still resounds in my mind. This was to make her feel special and to wish her a safe childbirth. When all the ladies in the room were done, they helped her rise to stand up and stretch her legs. She seemed relieved.

As a child, I could not understand why they did not do this for my mother, who was also pregnant at the time. Though the ladies brought special foods for her, the *Vyakku-koda* was celebrated only for the first pregnancy. I remember I still wished they would do the rituals for her, although it was her fifth pregnancy.

I was sad when I thought of how my mother, aunt, and sisters wouldn't be here in Chicago for a *vyakku-koda* for me. It made me homesick. I was totally surprised when my friends, Radha, Padma, and Sasi made some special foods and threw me a *Vyakku-koda* party.

I was so touched I was in tears, but these were happy tears.

Even in those days we tried to carry out our traditions despite the lack of Indian spices available to us. We bonded by helping each other with what little cooking skills each of us brought with us and celebrated each success with aplomb.

### Thursday, July 2nd, 1964

I noted in my diary, 'the little one moved within me for the first time." With the very first movement I knew it was the real thing. Not just a muscle twitch. Not just my imagination. I knew the little one was letting me know of her presence, and was demanding that I take good care of me so the care would be passed on to her. Of course, I did not know then It was a girl. The movement within me reminded me to take my vitamins and my calcium pills, and to drink milk every day, even if I lost some of it with my persistent morning sickness, which happened all through the day.

Lunchtime in the hospital cafeteria was quite intolerable. The sliced meat dishes and the smell of various sauces made me retch. I did not particularly like salads. Basically I survived on toast and tea. One afternoon, around 3:30 p.m., Vi, one of the food servers, came up to the pathology offices with a slice of pound cake and a small carton of milk. She insisted that I take a break and eat the cake, "We are all worried about you. In your condition, you need more nourishment. It is not good to go around hungry."

I burst into tears. Her act of kindness touched me. She took off her white cap, sat in the chair at the next desk, and wiped my tears with a tissue. She stayed with me and visited with Eleanor until I ate the cake and finished the milk.

When she left, Eleanor said to me, "Violet is so gruff and short-tempered in the cafeteria, I did not know she had this kindness in her. You're lucky."

At the end of the pregnancy, I had only gained nineteen pounds. I felt great. I worked until the day I had labor pains and went to the hospital.

A bit after midnight, in the early hours of December 12th, 1964, I felt the pain in my abdomen that heralded my little one's arrival. The pains came infrequently throughout the night. At 9:30 on Saturday morning I walked the two blocks over to the hospital, registered at the office, and admitted myself to the OB department in anticipation of my first childbirth. I had paged Raj when I got to the hospital but he did not answer. I was quite upset at the time. I found out later that he was at a departmental conference, and I forgave him.

At 11.03 p.m., almost 24 hours later, a beautiful little girl was born to us. The sight of her small face framed with dark, thick, almost curly hair made me laugh and cry at the same time. For her first official portrait, the nurse fastened a pink ribbon on her hair, but had to pin the hair off her face so her eyes would show in her photo.

I wondered how the distress that lasted almost a whole day was forgotten the minute the baby was placed in my hands? It could not be denial, because I knew the pain was real when it happened. But when her tiny fingers curled around my own, so much stronger than I ever imagined, somehow this sent signals to my brain to erase the agony of just moments ago. As her eyes met mine, the ecstasy I felt raised me to a higher plane and replaced the anxiety I felt from the many hours of labor and the possibility of a C-section I had heard discussed in the distant corners of the labor room.

Raj hugged us both, and I cried again. This time I cried because the miracle we created together had finally arrived.

We named her Devi, meaning 'goddess.' With such an auspicious name we were wishing her a great life.

Raj called home and gave our families the good news. I could not talk to my mother or grandmother because the baby and I stayed at the hospital for the next five days. I learned I could be lonely even in the midst of friends who visited me. Strangers stopped in my room to see the mother of the *'baby with so much hair.'*

When the nurse took the baby away from me to the nursery I was quite agitated because I could not have the baby with me all the time. Devi was brought to me for feedings, and the nurses frowned on my unwrapping the bundled infant so I could inspect her tiny toes and fingers and admire my little miracle.

Back home a newborn wore a cut out muslin top, and would lie next to the mother on a mat with a soft cloth for a sheet, and in those days there were no diapers. The adults stood around and commented on how agile the baby was when he/she would kick and scream. There were no scheduled feeding times; the baby would get fed anytime it screamed in hunger.

My loneliness and frustration increased. I wanted my mother and aunt to take care of me, not the strangers in this strange land where a mother was denied a chance to see her newborn naked. My friend, Padma, brought me our own brand of comfort food, rice and yogurt with lime pickle. It still was not enough.

Then, on the fourth day Raj brought me a pound of butterscotch candy, my favorite. For some reason my blues vanished as I shared the sweets with the nurses and my visitors, smiling through my tears.

I had suffered from post-partum depression, fortunately of a very mild degree.

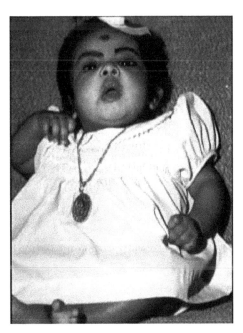

Baby Devi, January 1965.

# 30

## It Takes a Village To Raise A Child

**THE BABY NOW** took priority in my life. It was great to have friends who were closer to me than my family, not only physically but emotionally, since our family was at least 10,000 miles away. I considered Padma, Radha, and Sasi family because they were the ones who held me up emotionally. Sasi had a one-year-old baby boy, Radha had a two-year-old son, and Padma was big with baby. We did not know if it was a boy or girl. In those days ultrasound testing was not available to find out the baby's gender, so the mother found out when the baby was born.

Raj and I were fully aware that we held heavy responsibilities to raise the young ones back home at Hill View, so we decided I would return to work after four weeks of vacation. My eyes filled with tears at the thought of leaving my little Devi for whole work days. As it stood, I was getting paid for only two weeks of vacation time. There was no such thing as maternity leave. I was nostalgic for the practice back home of treating a new mother very special. When my ammachi had her babies she was given full paid maternity leave for three months. I wished I could stay home and enjoy my little girl for longer. If I had learned anything from my ammoomma it was to be practical, so I planned to return to work after four weeks.

On the 28th day after Devi's birth we had a naming ceremony for our baby girl. An oil lamp was lit, flowers and fruit were placed in front of it. I sat down on a folded blanket beside our holy setup. Wearing a cotton "mundu," wrapped around her little waist, she looked very Indian. For the first time in her life the baby was adorned with a classic pottu on her forehead, and her eyes were made up with black kohl. The kohl was even put on her eyebrows. As is usual on such occasion, she was showered with gifts. We adorned her with pieces of gold her grandparents had sent from India: a gold necklace, two gold rings, and a solid gold bracelet. In addition, she wore a gold waist chain braided in a classic design with tiny gold beads from Thankom Maami. This is known as an *'aranjanam,'* literally, an ornament for the waist. Back home she would wear it all the time until she was at least two years old.

Black plastic bangles were placed on both wrists. Padma tied a black thread on Devi's waist. Three spiral beads each about six millimeters long were made of three metals: bronze, copper, and silver, and were threaded on to Padma's thread. This is to balance the elements in the baby's system and to ward off evil spirits.

Now the naming started. Her aunt, Padma leaned down and whispered softly into her little ears her given name "Devi," three times. Then she picked her up from my arms. After hugs and kisses she returned Devi to my lap. Now it was Raj's turn. He did the same, naming her by calling "Devi," softly into her ears. Thus the little person was officially named. She was not just a baby girl, but "Devi." She was a little person, but a whole individual, big by her own right, a divine being all on her own. This is the ritual by which we *Malayalees* welcome our newly-born babies into this world.

Our friends also showered her with many gifts.

We gathered and had a feast of idlis, sambar, vadas, and *aravana payasam* made with rice, brown sugar and butter. The aravana payasam was a staple whenever we had ceremonies, including a pooja. I wished my sisters, Raj's sisters, and our parents could witness the special bundle of joy so honored, but was also thankful we had good friends who were there to bless her. Devi did not mind being passed from one aunt to the other, and a few minutes after she was fed she fell asleep amidst the food and conversation. Even though I missed my family back home, I tried to see the glass as half full, not half empty.

To this day, our first born daughter Devi has a very special place in the hearts of the remarkable friends who were more than family in our lives, and were the very first uncles and aunts who took pride in helping us raise her as an infant.

January1965, Shaku, Raj, Devi

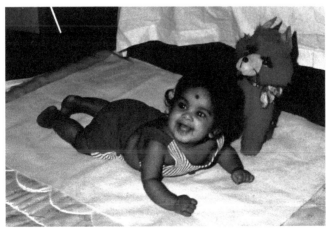

Photo # 28.    1965, Devi

1965 Spring.
Raj, Shaku and Devi at the Garfield Park Conservatory.

## *1965, A WARM SPRING DAY IN BERWYN, ILLINOIS*

Shaku, Devi,Padma, Kannan

Padma, Kannan, Shaku, Devi

Devi, Raj, Kannan, Shanmugham

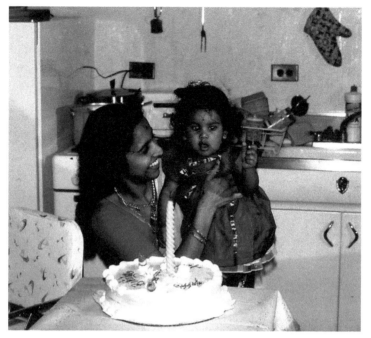

Devi's first Birthday

1966, Devi's second Birthday

1967, Devi's third Birthday

1967-12-12
1967 Devi's 3rd Birthday.

# 31

## Learning to Drive My Car

**I LEARNED TO** drive a car out of sheer necessity.

In the spring of 1965, Raj was accepted to start an Internal Medicine Residency in Mount Sinai Hospital in Chicago. We had to move by the end of June from the Gables in Berwyn to the residents' building, called the Kling Residence, near the hospital. No more daily rides for me to get to work. I had to drive my car if I wished to continue my own residency program at West Suburban Hospital.

Raj taught me how to drive our Impala. I was excited, as I usually am when I try anything new in my life. The lessons went smoothly, except when I changed lanes too close to the car to my right, or veered too close to the car in the left lane, and Raj gave me a hard knock on my head with his knuckles. I put up with that for a while, but when it came to parking I drew the line. I insisted on and received a professional training lesson. The trainer came to pick me up. To my chagrin he arrived in a huge Cadillac sedan which I was expected to drive. The ordeal shocked me to tears. The trainer, an elderly gentleman, put his arm on my shoulder in a conciliatory manner and said.

"Young lady, don't be upset. Once you learn to parallel park this car, you will never have trouble parking any other car."

So, off we went to a park in Maywood. There were long winding roads and many parking lots throughout this huge park. On our way to

Maywood from Berwyn, I drove on the Eisenhower Expressway. To this day I remember one piece of advice he gave me.

"Always keep an eye on the car two cars ahead of you. When you see red brake lights on that car you know you need to slow down. Because by the time the car immediately in front of you puts the brakes on, it is already too late to stop in time to avoid collision."

In the park he taught me to gauge the distance between parked cars and when to cut an angle for parking. After an hour of practice, I felt pretty confident. I did take a second lesson to polish upon my parking skills, and to go over the rules of the road with the kind gentleman. By the end of June I had mastered my driving skills. I received my driver's license just two days before I needed to go to work by myself. I was anxious, but not afraid to go it alone, because in the prior weeks I drove everywhere we went. Raj gave up the wheel so I could gain more experience. During my maiden voyage to work, I did feel a sense of freedom, and that felt good. Not because I was escaping from anything but because I did not have to depend on anybody to go for groceries or to attend any pathology meetings in town. I could even go buy my own clothes by myself.

I wished our driver, Krishnapillai Chettan, from the Chenthitta House was here to drive me to work. Excluding that possibility, I was glad, nay proud that I was able to drive our car to work. I was not the first woman in my family to drive a car. My sister Shanthi was living in Dar-e-Salaam in East Africa and had learned to drive a car earlier that year. I wrote home and I wrote to Shanthi of how liberated I felt driving my own car.

# 32

## The Snowstorm of the Century

**Thursday, January 27th, 1967**

AT 2:30 P.M., it was announced in the pathology department, (where I was a third year resident); anyone wishing to leave early could do so. A very intense snowstorm had hit the Chicago area. It had snowed non-stop for almost ten hours, and it was not expected to stop snowing for many more hours.

I hurried to complete as many cases as possible for the senior pathologist's review and left the department at 4:00 p.m.

My friends advised me not to drive home, because many of the streets were clogged by abandoned cars already. So, I walked the two blocks to the Lake Street El. I boarded the train going east, and settled down. About fifteen minutes later, when we approached California Avenue, I rose from my seat, ready to step out. But the train did not stop. The passenger next to me said I had taken the wrong train. There were A and B trains and I should have taken the other one to reach California Avenue. The next stop was Ashland. I stepped out.

Coming out of the train station, the size of the snowflakes combined with the speed of accumulation paralyzed me. I realized stopping in a commercial and warehouse area for shipping companies would not be a good idea, so I turned south and started walking toward Ogden

Avenue. I had a rough idea that it was a long walk, but did not know what else to do. Cars were stalled on the road and the buses were barely able to make it around the stalled cars. Even so, I called home to see if somehow Raj could come to pick me up. When I called from a pay phone, he described to me how no cars were getting by the corner of Ogden and California, where we lived. He was still recuperating from a bout of hepatitis and did not know how he could rescue me, even if he borrowed a friend's car. We decided I should keep walking and try to come home. If any buses were running, he said I should try to ride one. No buses were running to where I wanted to go.

I was already freezing, my boots stuck to my cold feet and I wished for a ray of my southern sun and an ounce of heat from my tropical home to thaw me out. I had never felt so far away from the warmth of my home, the caring hands of my mom my ammachi, and my maternal aunt. I started to pray. At first my head and my brain felt so frozen that I could not remember the words to my daily prayers. I kept repeating *"Hare Rama, hare Rama, rami rama hare hare.Hare Krishna, hare Krishna, Krishna Krishna, hare hare."* That was the simplest and the earliest prayer taught me as a youngster, and I kept repeating the two lines over and over again. After a while I was tromping on the snow-piled streets to the rhythm of my chanting. I was sobbing between my spoken words, when the snow blinded me and I fell flat on the road. Since no cars were moving, everyone had taken to the streets; the pavement was packed high with the onslaught of snow. A kind man helped me stand up from my fall. I thanked him and trudged on. It was certainly a good thing I had a sound sense of direction, and an accurate idea of where my apartment was located. As I regained my footing, I also regained my memory of words to more of my prayers. I kept chanting pieces of different prayers, and although still cold, I regained my strength to keep trodding along.

Eventually the tall building of our Kling residence was visible, and somehow I made it home. Raj was ready with warm rags to thaw out my toes and fingers, and quickly helped me out of my wet coat and wet clothes. Bundled up in blankets and propped up by pillows I told the story of my ordeal to my curious three-year-old. She felt my cold limbs and touched my cold face. Then she walked over to the picture window of our apartment, overlooking Ogden avenue, not really a picturesque sight, and banged on the window, saying "Bad snow, go away. Don't make my mummy cold." Righteous indignation from a sweet daughter.

I had a firm faith that our lives are part of a great cosmic plan, where all major events are really out of our individual control. This helped to make sense of the happenings of the day. While it was very upsetting, I gained insight into the workings of Mother Nature, and built a great strength within me after this experience. My walk in the snow in the bitter cold night of January, 1967 was a true test of faith.

My survival of the ordeal without losing a toe or a finger affirmed my faith in God. It affirmed the faith within me that I could face adversity without caving in to self-pity or turning bitter. It also affirmed my faith in those around me, even my young daughter who would speak up for me against Mother Nature's injustice.

# 33

## Nimmi, Our Second Born Arrives

*January 1970*

**I WAS AWAKENED** abruptly by abdominal pain around 2:30 a.m. I recognized the pain as the heralding of my second child's appearance. Ready or not she/he had decided to come two weeks earlier than I expected. The contractions were still far apart and not very painful. We waited until morning. Raj and I got ready for work and dressed Devi for school. We dropped Devi off with our upstairs friend, Rachel.

When I got pregnant with our second child we were more than ready. At least I knew what changes were happening in my body. I knew how to manage my cravings. I stocked up on hot curry masala and some genuinely red-pepper-hot pickles made of lime or green mangoes. The green mango pickles had to travel all the way from India, but the lime pickles were available in the two Indian grocery stores in Chicagoland. All foods, including MacDonald's hamburgers got a coating of lime pickle and red sauce between the buns. Just writing about it gets my saliva flowing. That is how strong and sour the pickled lime tastes.

I tried to reach my senior pathologist, (also my boss,) but he did not answer at home or at work. I reached my lab manager and she said Dr. K had not called. I knew I had to be there for frozen section diagnosis on a breast biopsy scheduled for 10:00 a.m. My labor pains were not frequent and with my history of really prolonged labor the first time, I was not worried about getting to the hospital on time. Raj dropped me off at work. The hospital I worked in was only twenty minutes from Mount Sinai Hospital in Chicago and I planned to take a cab after the patient's biopsy was done.

Dr. K did not come to work that morning. I completed the biopsy diagnosis on time. Then I called for a cab.

Meanwhile, I notified Mr. Singer, Chief Administrator, and Ms. Lee Kotnour, Chief of Nursing, that I had to leave to have my baby. Lee came to my office and assured me that I could be admitted right there if there was an impending labor. I assured her that I would be okay to take the cab to Mount Sinai Hospital. As luck would have it, no cabs came. I processed the specimens from surgery and kept busy with my slides for pathology diagnoses. An hour went by and no cab. My pains were twenty minutes apart. Merva Hand, my histology technologist decided she would drive me over. On the way I had a contraction and was in real pain. That scared Merva no end. I told her not to worry. If it got worse I could flag a policeman to escort us to Mount Sinai, fast.

Merva got me there safely, and I was admitted immediately. I paged Raj, who worked at University of Illinois Hospitals at the time and gave him a progress report. Once he knew I was safely admitted, he was in no hurry.

At 6:23 p.m. a little girl arrived kicking and screaming, announcing her presence on earth.

Raj was still not there. Our best friends, Padma and Shanmugam, stopped by to check on me from time to time.

When the nurse placed the baby girl in my arms, I felt I was in Heaven. She was so little. I hugged her tenderly and the warmth of my body and arms stopped her wailing. She was totally wrapped and bundled and I dreamily unwrapped her to count her toes and fingers. I was excited to see this little miracle to which I had given birth.

The nurse stopped me. I was shocked. I could not understand. She said I was not allowed to un-wrap the baby. I burst into tears. She did not even console me. She just took the baby from my arms and walked out, totally ruining my joyous moments with my newborn. I sobbed myself to sleep.

I don't know how much later Raj arrived, but he consoled me. Then he went to the nursery and spoke to the nurse in charge, convincing her to bring the baby back to my arms. Wearing a surgical gown, he helped me un-wrap her and allowed me to inspect the baby head to toe. Then he helped me feed her. I could not take my eyes off her. Pink cheeks, dark hair wavy upon the forehead and neck, little lips still sucking even as she fell asleep in my arms, and her chest moving gently with every breath; I cuddled her tight. I breathed a sigh of relief that the little one was perfect. I said my evening prayers as she lay comfortably in my arms. I wrapped her back into a cloth bundle and the nurse came and took her back to the nursery.

In the past year Devi, our firstborn, was included in all plans we made for the expected baby. Keeping her in the loop worked well because she herself accepted and anticipated the arrival of her sibling with great pleasure and hope.

Raj brought Devi with him to the hospital when he came to take me and the baby home. From the moment she saw the baby she took ownership as 'my baby sister.' All the way home Devi cuddled close to me and the baby as I held the baby on my lap. We didn't place newborns in car seats in those days.

Once home the three of us fussed over the little one. Each movement of her face, her first smile, her first bath at home, all was celebrated. When we said prayers at dusk Devi wished to hold her in her lap.

We sang songs to her. One of our favorites was by Karen Carpenter.

—"why do stars suddenly appear
every time— you are near—
Just like me—
They long to be— close to you—"

We named the little one **Nimmi.** It was a condensed version of Nirmala, meaning the innocent one and also one of the names of our Goddess Lekshmi.

Our five-year-old was excited about our new arrival as much as we the parents were expectant and excited.

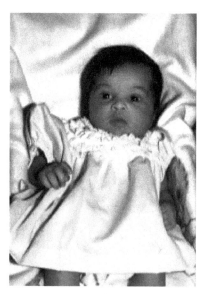

1970, Nimmi arrived bringing more joy.

1970, Devi holding on tight to her baby sister Nimmi.

# 34

## *My Last Job Interview*

**MY LAST JOB** interview was at Westlake Community Hospital in May, 1970.

The pathologists from West Suburban Hospital were covering the pathology services at Westlake for a couple of years, and I, as a resident under them, worked on some cases there. I was familiar with the way the laboratory and pathology services functioned at Westlake, and when the position for "Pathologist and Director of Laboratories," opened up, I applied for it.

Although I was only one year out of training and had lived in this country for only six years, I knew I was qualified to perform in both roles. I had been trained by the best. Dr. Geoffery Kent was not only a leader in his field, he was such an effective chief of the pathology department, that I considered myself fortunate to see a master in action. When a physician needed special tests for a problem patient, Kent pulled all stops to get them done.

When a doctor on the staff was unhappy about test results and blamed a member of the laboratory staff, not only did Dr. Kent solve the problem effectively, he always defended the staff member if he was in the right. If a staff member made a mistake, the staff member was reprimanded, but never in the presence of others, and never in a mean way.

If Dr. Kent was not sure of what procedure needed to be performed to clarify a diagnosis on tissue removed from surgery, he did not hesitate to request a consultation from a specialist, even if the answer required came from specialists in Washington or New York. I felt privileged to speak to some of the best pathologists in the country when they were handling Dr. Kent's cases in consultation, like Dr. Hans Popper, the most famous liver pathologist of the time.

I knew in my heart the training I had experienced under my ammoomma, and the discipline she used to manage her practice and her family, including the habits she inculcated in me, would guide me if I took on such a responsibility. I also knew that the compassion my father showed in his life would stand as a beacon for me to follow in my career as a physician and a pathologist.

After a tour of the hospital, the laboratory, and pathology departments, Mrs. Elsie Willard, Chief Administrator and I sat talking in her office.

"Dr. Shaku, what are you doing here?" A familiar voice broke into our conversation and Dr. Nicholas came up to me and gave me a hug.

Mrs. Willard explained to him I was interested in the pathologist and director of the laboratories position. Dr. Nicholas wished me luck and left.

About 7:00 the same night Mrs. Willard called.

"Dr. Shaku, I wish to offer you the job at my hospital. Can you stop by tomorrow afternoon so we can discuss the details?"

I was in a daze. "I can come after three o'clock. Will that be too late?" I asked.

"That will be fine."

We hung up. I did not realize what a life-altering few words those were.

Later I found out that as soon as Dr. Nicholas reached his office, he called Mrs. Willard and said to her, *"If Dr. Shaku is interested in the job, grab her. She is the best."* Dr. Nicholas was a senior member of the staff at Westlake at the time, and had performed surgery there for over twenty years. His was all the recommendation she needed to place her confidence in me. He knew me and my work from West Suburban Hospital, and had complimented me on more than one occasion about how thorough I was, and how well I 'operated' on the body of whoever I was doing an autopsy on.

I accepted the job and started my career as Pathologist and Director of Anatomic Pathology and Clinical Laboratory at Westlake Community Hospital on June 1st, 1970

I retired from there on November 30th, 1998, after twenty-eight-and-a half-years. The people I met, the cases I saw, the patients whose lives I touched directly or indirectly, all helped form the person that I have become.

In all the years in between I raised three girls, helped form the future of the department by hiring many technologists, clerical, and support personnel, and unfortunately had to fire a few.

When a person perfectly qualified for a particular job fails to perform, I am convinced the system the leaders set up is partly to blame. I, in all honesty, tried to be fair to judge the ones for only their part in the failure. Making anyone a scapegoat for a problem not totally under one's control was never acceptable. I have had to make difficult choices to comply with rules and laws that existed.

In 1971, abortion was illegal in Illinois, unless under certain circumstances. All tests done in my laboratory had to be under the order (request) of a physician. There was a phlebotomist who had the authority to draw blood, and did not have the training or the job-permission to perform a pregnancy test, yet did her friend a 'favor' and tested her friend's urine. Results showed the lady was pregnant. Based on the test, the lady went on to New York and obtained an abortion; it was legal there. When I found out what had happened, the disciplinary action was to fire the phlebotomist for doing the test without a doctor's request. It was indeed sad to let a very good phlebotomist go; however, she had performed an unauthorized function. I had no choice.

I know many people who read this book will be surprised that doing autopsies on the dead bodies of patients did not bother me. In the days when I started my pathology practice, CAT scans, MRIs, and other sophisticated testing were not available. The final cause of death could only be decided by doing an autopsy, thus revealing the cause of death. As hard as it was to convince families to agree, the attending physicians tried hard to convince the immediate relatives to consent to an autopsy. Once we found the reason for the death, the families were usually thankful we did the autopsy.

Sometimes doing this post-mortem examination was hard on me as when I had to do one on a fellow physician who died of a brain tumor. This particular doctor acted bizarre at his daughter's wedding and had to be admitted to the hospital. The tests showed he had a brain tumor, and when the surgeon opened his skull there was a golf ball sized tumor in his brain. After the tumor was removed he seemed to improve, but soon afterwards he had complications and he died. Upon doing the autopsy I found the tumor had spread between the lobes of the brain and caused blood clots in some vessels, which led to his demise. There was no way to find this with the test methods available to the doctors. This is one of those cases when the autopsy was really necessary. It was hard on me to dissect the body of one who was well known to me, yet it was my duty to help find answers. So I did.

Just one month after I started my job at Westlake I took the initiative and convened with the chief of radiology, the chairman of the surgery department, the main oncologist on our Medical Staff, to start a **tumor board** at Westlake Hospital. This board met two times a month and arranged for conferences to discuss all cancer cases at our hospital. The attending physicians were invited to present the patient and the details of diagnosis. In addition I, as pathologist, the radiologist and any other doctor involved in the case discussed the patient's workup and treatment. The oncologist, the surgical specialist and other physicians present contributed to the discussion, thus improving patient care. This also brought forward research and new treatment options to the rest of the medical staff. Current testing necessary for deciding optimal treatments were instituted in the laboratory and radiology departments as a result of such open reviews of the various types of cancer. We also took advantage of the cutting edge research going on in the university hospitals in town and arranged for consultants from such hospitals to come to our Tumor Board sessions. This really improved the chances of survival of our cancer patients.

1970, July. Family portrait. Devi, Nimmi, Dr. Shaku and Dr. Raj. Published in the Daily Herald and Pioneer Press publications, announcing Dr. Shaku as the new Director of Pathology and Clinical Laboratories at Westlake Community Hospital.

# 35

## A Career Begins

I **KNEW EXACTLY** what was expected of me as a *Pathologist and the Director of Pathology and Clinical Laboratories.*

Would I have the courage and wisdom to do it? The questions kept me awake on many nights. Was I too young to handle the demands the older physicians would be placing on me?

In those moments I comforted and reassured myself: "All I have to do is concentrate on doing the right thing by each patient, do it in the name of God, and let God take care of the rest." As if my conscience spoke, I realized I needed to be careful not to be too sure of myself or take chances on a diagnosis. If I had any doubts in making a diagnosis when I looked at a biopsy through the microscope, I had to ask for help. And I knew I had to always explain to the attending physician why I requested a consultation on certain of the cases. It was crucial to maintain the trust element with the doctors at all times.

I was the only pathologist in the hospital and there was no one else at the next microscope to look at cases with me. I was afloat on high seas and my nautical skills were being tested.

The fact that I had confidence in myself to face such a challenge came from the trust and responsibility that doctors such as Dr. Kent, Dr. Volini, Dr. Orfei, and Dr. Battifora placed in me.

I also felt empowered by the knowledge I gained in working with

Dr. Robert Muehrcke, an Internist and Nephrologist who had great trust in the way I handled his kidney biopsies, and in the way I presented the diagnostic methodology to his medical residents.

For the weekly tumor board sessions, where cancer cases were discussed and treatment protocols decided, I was the only resident allowed to present the cases. All the others were attending physicians whose patients were being discussed. The confidence Dr. Kent placed in my ability to discuss a case may not be by itself a big deal, but I know it was many years later that other residents were included in the tumor board discussion panel.

I had the privilege of learning brain pathology with Dr. Manny Ross at Northwestern University. For many months I went to his neuropathology lab to study thin slices of brain and identify the pathological changes. This was followed by microscopic study of the same areas to complete the diagnostic process. In our electron microscopic lab I learned how important it was to sample the proper area of any organ to see diagnostic changes when the pictures were taken from the electron microscope. I knew in my heart I had seen and diagnosed enough cases of liver diseases to acknowledge when the scope of diagnosis needed expert help.

I had good friends among the experienced pathologists who trained me. Many of the specialists in town were known to me. All I had to do was call them up and either drive over to the hospital in Chicago with my slides or put the slides with a courier service to cab them over, and could easily obtain a consultation and a second opinion on any case, and the best part was that the patient did not receive another bill from the consultant because it was done as a favor to me. If the patient then went to another hospital for further care, the consultant would of course see and bill them.

I had to search deep within myself and find enough strength to make the system work, and yet change whatever was not working in the system.

The Clinical Laboratory at Westlake did not have a regular schedule for night shift coverage, because administration did not want to spend money on a technologist to be there if the emergency room was not busy. I immediately undertook a study of how many times the inpatients needed help at night, but had to wait until the next morning for their tests to be done. I also studied the extra expense spent on overtime pay when the day shift personal ended up working extra on 'as needed' basis.

Based on my cost analysis and justification of patient needs a night shift was instituted soon after.

The doctors on the staff were happy with the improvement in patient care. That was just the beginning of my association with Westlake Community Hospital, one that was mutually beneficial, and one that took us both to heights of satisfactory patient care, while maintaining high standards in the running of a laboratory, for a long time to come.

# 36

## The Blue Saree

THE PHOTO ON the wall has beckoned me to write about my life beginning thirty-two years ago when our family posed for a studio portrait.

My husband stood tall on the right side of our family, ever the protector, often the over-protector. His eyes asked for more, more out of life as he looked forward, ready to be photographed.

Our first born girl, Devi, who had turned six, was nestled between her dad and me. She smiled with confidence. Her long wavy hair flowed over both shoulders, her bangs covered her forehead and were in slight disarray, thanks to the busy fingers of her eleven-month--old sister who rested on my arms.

To the left of the picture, I sat holding our eleven-month-old daughter Nimmi. My head was cocked to the left, leaning toward the baby. I looked forward, but out of the corner of my eyes. I smiled--a smile that says I love this world. This world of mine with my Balu Chettan (that is what I called my husband), my dear Devi-mol, and our little rascal, Nimmi-mol.

The baby held on to my saree, between my bosoms, which wrinkled my attempt at perfect pleats over my shoulder. I didn't seem to mind. Then again I did not even mind if my girls interrupted my perfectly planned schedules.

Back to the baby. She cocked her head to her right, and leaned her forehead against mine. Propped up on my left arm, she cuddled between her older sister and me. The tentative smile on her face revealed that she was not certain if she wanted to smile at the stranger who pointed a big black camera at us. Yet, confident of her safety in my arms, she tendered a sly smile. "*Konchi*," that is our Malayalam word for the coquettish, impish smile and behavior when children win us over without really trying.

When my daughter, Devi, was twelve she made the wise remark, "There is no English word for the term *Konchi*; is there? That is the only way to describe what Nimmi does. Right, Mom?" I agreed with her. The look on our eleven-month-old's face, with the bent neck and eyes that look so dreamy made me want to kiss them, which can only be described as *Konchi*.

The blue pure silk saree with a red border reminds me of our life back then. We had left our home in Trivandrum, South India in 1964. This photo was taken in December 1970, and we still had not gone back to visit. I missed my sisters. I missed seeing my brother. I missed talking to Ammachi, my favorite aunt. I missed my mother and my grandmother. I was still hurting and haunted that I had not said goodbye to my step-great-grandmother, who was my special '*cater-to-Paapa person*," (Paapa was my pet-name), while I grew up.

Most of all, I missed my father–my daddy. I saw him for the last time in January, 1964, when he saw me off as I boarded a TWA flight from Bombay, leaving India to join my Balu Chettan, who was already living in Berwyn, Illinois.

If I knew then that it would be my last time I see Daddy, would I have said, '*I love you forever*'? I don't know. I don't know if I said, *I love you, Daddy*. I know I leaned down and touched his feet to receive his blessings for my journey. I did not know I would not touch those feet ever again. I did not know that the blessings he gave me would need to last me a lifetime. Maybe it was better that I did not know. I love you, Daddy. I was all of 23 years old then. Who thinks of death and dying when one is that young? My daddy died in September 1970.

The picture on the wall reminds me of how I complained that I hadn't bought one new *"pure-silk"* saree in seven years. All my blouses were getting frayed, and some were tight after two child-births. The gripe about the saree was the tip of the iceberg that was chilling my heart and spirit; the death of my dad in September had really affected me badly.

Then, one day a parcel came in the mail, all the way from Trivandrum, India. The postmark showed it cost a hefty Rs.95.00 (Rupees), quite a large sum for a package by air.

I tore through the wrappings and found a blue silk saree with a gold and red border. It was made of pure silk. A note was attached from our brother-in-law, Ramachandran, it read, *"hoped that Paapa would like it."* My husband, Balu Chettan, had unbeknownst to me, sent a money-order for a saree and surprised me with it, air-mail and all. For all the brusque retorts to my previous complaints: *"Why do you have to go back?"* and *"Why can't you just buy a nylon saree here?"* he had taken the trouble to procure a pure silk saree for me. My smile in the picture showed that it helped. I sewed a blouse in matching blue, myself. There was no 'Tailor Madhavan' around the corner to make it for me overnight. When I talked my husband into having our portrait taken that December, I did wear the blue saree with the red border.

The blue saree did not help me miss my family back home any less, but it made me realize that cherishing the family I have here is what

life is about. I am not sure if I thanked him enough, then. I do thank him now. And I thank God for all my human bounty.

The picture on the wall, December, 1970 Shaku, Nimmi, Devi, Raj.

# 37

## Our Decision to Stay

**OUR LITTLE GIRL** was tucked away in her crib, the dinner dishes were put away, and Raj and I were comfortably seated on our bed, three pillows lifting our heads as we perused the library materials we needed for our assignments the next day. We needed to be well prepared to present our cases to our immediate senior doctors. In addition, we had different responsibilities when describing our cases to the rest of the members of respective departments, with thorough analysis, diagnosis, and suggested treatments. We read our textbooks deep into the night to be well versed on the diagnosis and treatment of the respective patients we were to discuss.

Out of the blue, Raj said. "I want us to think about staying in America for good."

"What?" I sat straight up. "How about our parents? Your mom, my dad, Mom, Ammachi and Ammoomma? How about all the kids at home we still have to raise? Who will take care of them if we don't return home?"

"My Uncle Appu-Annan is staying with Mom and the young ones now. And he will continue to help my mom with them. Besides, if we stay here we will be able to send enough money to support Mom and help her raise all the kids at home. And, anyway, we don't have to decide right now but I want you to consider the possibilities."

I could not concentrate on my reading and did not get much sleep that night. I missed my dad and my mom, and everybody else, but even more disturbing was the thought that we would not be setting up our practices in Trivandrum, and offer free service to the indigent in the hospital clinics as my father wished we would. If Kesavan Maaman was still alive, that is what he would want Raj, his son, to do as well.

The initial shock of the idea to stay in America whirled around in my head, and I could not concentrate on my cases or my lectures for days to come.

A few days later Raj was pleading his case with me, stating that if we stayed, he could use his skills learning cutting edge medicine and how modern advances in diagnosis could help him in his practice. When I argued against it, he assured me we would do more good by sending money back home for our family and also could help with the care of poor people in our town.

I was in tears. I saw it was hopeless to fight about it. I understood how the responsibility of providing for eight siblings and his mom weighed heavily on him. Although Mom owned rice fields and some properties, they did not provide a steady income supporting the family. I also knew that for the field to produce, we had to invest in the farmer and the farming process to yield enough rice for the family to live on.

I tried to tell Raj we could both set up practice back home, and if we worked hard we could make an ample income to raise the family.

His argument went on that here the billing system was set up so he did not need to discuss money with his patients, nor did he need to take cash from a patient personally. Finally I said, "Do what you want to do. I don't want to hear about it."

Seeing how the topic upset me he did not bring it up any more.

Then one day when thumbing through our mail, I saw a receipt for our application to receive a resident visa, and procuring a "green card." I was stunned. It became clear we were staying here permanently.

I was not happy about it and refused to discuss the topic with Raj for a long time. As upset as I was about the decision, I saw how Raj was trying to be the practical one. I realized he wished to be with his mother and his siblings the same way I wished with my family. But he based his decision on the economics of raising the young family at Hill View and still having a comfortable family life for us here. I could not leave my emotions out; yet I honoured his practical sentiments and stopped arguing about it.

One thing I made clear to him. I was not going to cry about the situation anymore. I was going to work as hard as needed to make the best of what fate handed me. I was determined to have the best of both worlds.

# 38

## My New Country

**WAS IT FATE** that brought me and planted me in this fertile land called America? Was it fate that separated me from my beloved people and bestowed upon me the arduous task of growing and prospering in this country? I do believe in fate but I am not fatalistic. I do believe many events in life are determined by fate, but I don't believe they cannot be altered by our actions based on our experience, our knowledge, and intuition.

One thing I knew for sure, this move of 10,000 miles from home, change of residence and the challenges in front of me were meant to test my fortitude and my resilience. Each day brought a new task or a new test. The multiple jobs of a full time pathology resident, a part-time lab technologist, (doing cytology screening of PAP-smears for cancer cell changes to make a little spending money,) full-time mother, and a dutiful wife were piling up heavy on my plate. With youth in my corner, a work ethic handed down through maternal and paternal DNA, and a heart steeped in optimism, I managed alongside my husband, Raj, to live a fulfilled life.

But then things happen over which one has no control.

My four-year-old, Devi, woke up one morning with a fever and intense coughing. I could not take her to nursery school. I had assignments at work I could not postpone, and Raj was working at the emergency department and unable to take the day off. It was a true dilemma. My father used to say; "*Eshwaran*, God, will find a way." Then I remembered Jaya.

One month prior I had met a young lady, Jaya, from my hometown who had just moved to the Chicago area. She was the wife of a Malayalee lab technologist working at West Suburban Hospital where I still worked. I had welcomed her and made friends with her when she arrived in this country. She was homesick just as I was when I first arrived. Knowing she was settling in at her new home, I called and asked her for a favor. Jaya graciously agreed to care for Devi until her fever subsided and Devi could go back to nursery school. Making new friends was easy for me. I learned that no human contact is ever wasted. I had helped Jaya feel at home when she was homesick; maybe fate played its hand for her to now help me.

When we decided to live here, I also decided to make myself at home. I said repeatedly, "I will have the best of both worlds." Raj and I adapted to the various foods we had never tasted before: hamburgers, hot dogs, different kinds of cheese, and even the different breakfast cereals. When I left Trivandrum, we had cornflakes available in the stores, but in my home the cornflakes were garnished with onions, green and red peppers, fried mustard seeds, fresh ginger, and shredded fresh coconuts. Such a dish was called *uppumavu*. So the cornflakes became a spicy Indian breakfast dish.

By transplanting our lives in America from a very rich Indian culture we were interested in participating in cultural programs, and visiting the museums and art galleries in the Chicagoland area. Our friends Padma and Shanmughom, and Raj Sekharan, joined us as we explored those special places. We visited the Garfield Park Conservatory, especially on the occasion of the spring flower show and Easter-lily-time. The blooming lilies spread their perfume around me like a long arm of comfort reaching out to me from all the way across the oceans, caressing me and imbuing me with strength to handle many problems we had to face, such as my morning sickness with my second pregnancy.

In my mode of Americanization, I learned Xmas songs so I could teach Devi the words. My friend, Marge from work wrote down the words to all the Xmas songs to help me learn them. She had a young daughter about Devi's age so I made the effort to join the two girls together for playtime. Raj and I grew our own adopted families among our colleagues here. Between the job responsibilities and raising our own family, the heaviness of the homesickness seemed to abate. Yet, a dull ache remained deep in my heart due to the longing for the warmth of my mother's hugs, my father's smile, my ammoomma's strict voice, and Ammachi's reading books with me. The thoughts of my seniors took me back all those miles and reduced me to a child of seven or eight again.

Slowly but surely the Indian community grew each year in the Chicago area. We made extra efforts to meet and help each other, especially with information regarding obtaining Indian vegetables such as yucca and Indian spices. We gathered and celebrated our children. We celebrated our Indian cultural holidays the best we could without a temple to go to for special offerings. American holiday traditions were also honored and celebrated. Unknowingly we were building our own family structure in this adoptive land of ours.

# 39

## A Dozen Red Roses Across the Seven Seas for Me, His Daughter

**On October 1,** 1964, I opened the door to my apartment, and there was Raj holding a vase of red roses and smiling ear to ear. My first response was to gush and thank him for the flowers. Then he told me with a guilty grin, "I can't take credit for these. Your Daddy sent them."

"All the way from India? How could he do that?" I was confused.

"Of course he ordered them in India, you silly girl." My husband really knew how to push my buttons.

"I am not silly. I just don't get it. When we place a phone call we don't even get through to India on the first try. How did he manage to send the roses to me on my birthday?"

It was incredible that my father had really sent a dozen red roses for my twenty-fourth birthday, all the way across seven seas and four continents.

I was crying now. It was my first birthday away from home. I missed the *payasam*, a sweet porridge-like dessert we made on all special days, especially birthdays. This would have been the year that my mother, my mother-in-law, and my ammachi would have made three different kinds. My maami would make *ada-payasam* with flat rice noodles, brown sugar, and coconut milk. My mom would make a *paal-payasam* with rice grains and sugar in whole milk, stirring patiently over a hot stove for over ninety minutes, while the milk simmered slowly to a rose color from the partial caramelization of the abundant sugar put in it. Ammachi would make *kadala-payasam*, with split lentils of the special kind of yellow peas, again simmered with brown sugar and coconut milk. Each kind warranted different levels of flavoring with crushed cardamom powder. I loved all three payasams, and loved all three ladies even more.

If I were back home, I would take an early bath and go to Chenthitta Devi temple for blessings from the Goddess Parvathi, the main deity there and stop by to see Ammoomma and Ammachi. The warm kadala-payasam would be waiting for me and Ammachi would sit across the dining table watching me eat the payasam. As usual, her eyes would fill with tears that could flow down her cheeks any second. Ammachi cried when she was sad, and when she was happy. Oh, how I missed her tears.

I would then stay at the Chenthitta house until lunch time. Walking into my Mom's home I could expect loud singing of "happy birthday" by my two sisters and my only brother, and loud clapping while Mom stood behind them, smiling silently. It was her first-born coming home to celebrate a birthday with her. It would be no surprise that she allowed my siblings to cut classes to enjoy my birthday. My dad would not oppose it either. We would share lunch and talk about school and work, and tease Mom about her lack of culinary skills. I know she would hug me and say that she really stirred the milk for a long time to make my paal-payasam. She always had help in the kitchen, but for my birthday treat she would do it all by herself.

When I was around, nobody was allowed to take a siesta. I dragged them all out for a walk by the tree-lined streets near Mom's home. Dad and I walked quite fast even after a full lunch. The others walked a little slower. When we returned, I had to say goodbye and go back to my new home with Raj's mother at Hill View.

The whole gang including my six sisters-in-law, two brothers-in-law, and Thankom Maami would be thrilled to see me return home and eager to share a special meal with me as well as my special treat, the ada-payasam. They made me feel very special too. It was always a difficult decision which little person got to sit by their newly acquired sister-in-law at dinner-time.

The memories brought a new flood of tears, I was seven months pregnant, making every experience more acute. While I cried for them and the payasam I was missing, my husband kept talking.

"Your father is the craziest person I know. These flowers are expensive. Even if I had the money, I would not waste it to send flowers all the way across the world."

Quickly wiping my tears, I turned around. "Of course you wouldn't," I said. Now I was smiling broadly and glowing in the thought of my crazy father and his love for his first-born daughter, separated from him for the first time ever, on her birthday. I had taken it for granted that he would always be there, as in all my previous birthdays when he brought me the *prasadams* from the temple to bless me.

In later years, with a busy life as a practicing physician and raising three daughters, there would be little time for nostalgia. But I did take the time and effort to show my girls photographs of their immediate family back in India, and told them stories of the kind Appooppa waiting to meet them.

We could not travel to India because when we applied for our immigrant visa, our training visa status was in a suspended state until a decision was made; and that took over five years. By the time we finally could visit, my girls were seven and two years old.

My father was a visionary who thought that by being generous, he could make others generous too.

I remember he only wore Khadi cloth, homespun coarse cotton

which Mahatma Gandhi supported and promoted as part of his anti-British movement. My father was a true Gandhian follower. He wore these clothes to instill pride of Indian-made clothing and to boycott British-made suits and pants.

Even at the age of five, I had to spin cotton on a *Charka* which had a base you steadied with your feet. I turned the wheel using one arm, while the other arm fed cotton to the sharp tip and gently pulled it so the cotton thread was generated. The thread was then twisted into skeins and Dad took them to the khadi board and sent to the mills for producing the cloth. When I was a child only white cloth was made from that thread. Later I saw the khadi cloth dyed with saffron color for the holy men and women at the ashrams, special Hindu monasteries. Nowadays the coarse cloth is treated to make it soft and khadi-silk is made into sarees and various fancy outfits.

When I started school, he enrolled me in Holy Angels Convent School, run by a French order of nuns. From kindergarten through high school I was educated in English. Dad was steadfast in his desire that I learn to think, write, and speak in English so that I would be more effective in fighting and getting rid of the British.

Among the books he inspired me to read was *Discovery of India,* by Pandit Jawaharlal Nehru, a freedom fighter and right hand to Mahatma Gandhi. This particular book was a compendium of letters that Nehru wrote to his daughter, Indira; it covered the growth and history of India, and why it was important that we break free from British rule. My father discussed how Gandhiji and Nehru, along with the Mohammadan leader, Jinnah, led our people against the British to free India. At the age of seven, I did not quite grasp the ideas, though Nehru's love toward his daughter Indira, and his love of his country, India, were palpable.

My dad not only gave me the book, he also took me to the theatre on Sunday afternoons to a program called 'visual education.' I saw film clips of Gandhiji wearing his minimal white cloth outfit and wooden sandals, sitting across the huge conference table in London from the British leaders in their wool suits and polished shoes. He held his own, while demanding freedom for his people. He was conspicuous in his humility, and in the determination and strength of his conviction. I watched with wonder how fast he moved from the car to the conference table, using a walking stick to keep his balance. His voice and his gestures reflected his impatience at how slowly the British were moving. Some of the scenes showed his anger at British efforts to hang on to trade privilege in India. Other times he wept openly when he pleaded with our Muslim counterparts, led by Jinnah, and with the British leaders, not to split India and Pakistan into two nations. Other film clips showed his fasting and demonstrating against **the split** and how weak he became, not having eaten for many days in protest of the procrastination by the British.

Indian Independence Day, August 15, 2018

Seventy-one years ago my sister Shanthi and I, alongside our cousins, were allowed to stay up until midnight to hear the celebration on the radio of:

The Birth Of a New Nation, an Independent India.

The national anthem blasted over the radio at midnight. I sang along, as best as I could at seven years old. I don't think I knew all the words. But I remember my little heart pounding with pride as my father cheered me on.

The next day we watched the Independence Day Parade at the Pangode Military Base, not too far from town. We were handed little tricolor flags of a free India to wave as the parade passed by the viewing stands.

In the year previous to this event, Mahatma Gandhi had tried his level best to avoid splitting India into the two countries of India and Pakistan. In support of Mahatma, my father, photographer Sivaraam, who was an ardent Gandhian follower, posted the tableaux below in the local paper as an illustration to keep the two countries together. With the relief of a 'United India-Pakistan' in the background, I donned a Nehru-cap and touted the Indian flag, while Shanthi had the muslim salwar-kameez outfit and the flag of Pakistan. The accompanying article pleaded with our leaders not to split the two countries.

While both attained freedom from the British rule, history has shown that the state of India and Pakistan as one united nation was not meant to be.

Freedom fight, 1946-1947
*On the relief of a united India-Pakistan country, Shaku wearing a Nehru-cap holding an Indian flag, and Shanthi with the Muslim Salwaar-Kameez outfit holding a Pakistani flag. This was the local town's appeal to avoid splitting the two nations. It did not come to fruition.*

The Indian Flag

My loyalty to the land of my origin was not by happenstance. It was seeded and grown by the beliefs of a dedicated father who wished to see me grow up in a free India. But in matters of the heart, neither of us had any control. When I fell in love with Raj, I decided to follow him here to the United States, and plant our future here as per his wishes. I know I hurt my dad and his dreams for me. By then India was a strong, fast-growing, independent nation, and did not need me to fight for its freedom. However, I know my dad still needed me. I was too young and naïve to realize how much until it was too late. Dad had wished for me to return and practice medicine dedicated to serving the poor. I would have been happy doing that. Except that Fate intended my life to be here, in the U.S.A. and totally intertwined with my husband's dharma. I accepted that with grace and love.

1965, K.V. Sivaraam, my dad.

# 40

## *Glimpses of Mortality*

IN SEPTEMBER OF 1970, in Park Ridge, Illinois, the telephone rang. It was Olga, my secretary, calling from my office. It was my day off. What did she want now? It was a Tuesday afternoon in Chicago, and it was my half-day off from work. Raj had joined me and our two girls for a late lunch at McDonald's, after which we had gone grocery shopping. I had duly changed our wet eight-month-old, set her in her playpen with her plush toys, and turned on the television to some children's program. Our six-year-old had three playmates over and the house rang loud with their chatter and laughter while they played hide and go seek. Raj had left to make a quick stop at the bank.

"Dr. Shaku, I have a telegram here." Olga's voice sounded different. "Your old neighbor, Rachel, called me and I just picked it up from the telegraph office."

We had only moved to Park Ridge from Oak Park three months prior, and all my immediate family in India knew my new address. What had happened? Who was trying to contact me?

"Okay, Olga, read it to me," I urged, my heart up in my throat and my voice hoarse. Telegrams were always ominous.

"Can I bring it to you?"

"No, Olga. It is too far to come. Just read it to me."

Her voice was hesitant.

*"Daddy passed away Monday A.M. (stop). Could not reach you by phone. (stop). Call TVM (Trivandrum) as soon as you can."*

*Signed Toby.*

Toby was my brother-in-law. Daddy could only mean my daddy. I thought he had come home from the hospital four weeks ago following a heart attack, and that he was stable.

"Doctor Shaku, are you there?" Olga's voice brought me back. She was crying.

"Yes, yes." I spoke mechanically. "Olga, thanks for calling me."

"Will you be okay? Is your husband home?" She did not want to hang up.

"He'll be home soon. The kids are here. I'll be okay."

It was Tuesday at 3:00 p.m. It would be Wednesday at 1:00 a.m. back home. Daddy had met his maker two days ago and I did not even know it. For a minute I could not find my voice.

"Doctor, are you all right?" Olga remained on the other end of the telephone I held to my ear.

"I am not all right. But I will be. Thank you for calling."

"I am so sorry, doctor." Olga hung up.

I must have screamed, because my daughter Devi came running into the kitchen.

"My daddy, your Appooppan, died. I have to call my mommy." I explained to her that I was very sad because I would not see my dad ever again. She hugged me tight. I felt the love she had for me in that mighty hug.

Then she said, "Mommy, turn off the rice pot and sit down."

Even at that tense moment her safety training came through. I had forgotten I'd started cooking rice for our dinner.

I obeyed her request and sat down.

She sat down beside me, as I sat sobbing on the floor. She cradled me in her little arms, and rocked me back and forth as best she could, just as I had rocked her in the past to soothe her when she fell or got hurt in any way.

The rocking motion is one that calms. The instinct to comfort and the universal physical movements are inherent. There was no need to teach a lesson as to what had to be done. If only we could nurture these instincts in more of our children, maybe we could avoid wars.

Devi then stood up and went to her sister Nimmi in the living room. I heard her talking with her three friends, who she asked to speak softly. They turned the volume low on the television, and then Devi came back to the kitchen.

"Daddy will be right back, Mom. Please don't cry," she repeated, clinging to me and in tears herself.

I had not seen my father for almost seven years, not due to any fault of mine. But still the fact remained that I had not seen him. I collected myself, picked up the phone, and booked a long-distance call to India. In those days one had to 'book' a call and wait for at least two hours to get connected.

My mind would not stop replaying memories of my father, and the telegram news. I had spoken to Dad about two months prior for only a few minutes. We never extended our phone calls more than the first three minutes because it cost too much after that. His firm voice resonated in my ears. "Yenta ponnu-molé," he had addressed me. "Golden daughter." He was the one who steadied me when my voice faltered during my phone call.

My husband came home while I was still in the kitchen. The kitchen was the only room with a telephone and I had to stay there till my mom called. "Daddy," I heard Devi say to him. "Appooppan died yesterday. Mommy just found out."

He dropped the packages he carried and rushed to my side. He held me close and said. "Did you call your mom yet?"

"I have placed the call."

"Come lie down on the couch," he coaxed me.

"No," I sobbed, "the telephone will ring any time."

It seemed like an eternity before it finally rang. My sister's teary voice came on the phone. "Paapchi, he's gone." She could not speak anymore. Then Toby took the phone from her.

"Yes, Paapa, The cremation is over," Toby said. It is 2:00 a.m. on

Wednesday here, and since we could not reach you on Monday and Tuesday, we had to go ahead with the rituals."

As was customary in our part of the world, and according to Hindu tradition, my father's body should have been cremated before sundown on Monday. The family was fully aware that I would not make it back for at least two whole days. They were not even sure if I'd received the telegram in time. So, although they waited to hear from me for over a day, they had to proceed with the cremation by the end of the day on Tuesday, their time. What they did not know was that I had not even been notified until that very day.

"I know Toby. I do understand." I replied, my voice steady now. "What happened?"

"Dad was getting ready to go to his photo studio. He had finished breakfast, and was in his easy-chair waiting for amma to bring him his *jubba* that she was ironing. When amma returned with his *jubba*, he was not breathing. We took him to the hospital immediately. But, it was already too late."

"At least he did not suffer long." I said through my sobs and wails. "Can Amma talk to me?"

"She wants to talk to you. Here she is," Toby said.

"Paapa, my light is gone to his Lord Narayana. He has left us all behind." My amma sounded so brave.

"What happened, Amma?" I was loud and out of control. The firm fingers of my husband on my shoulders did nothing to calm me down.

My mother was the strong one. "He is gone from this earth, môl, but he will be with us forever. Don't cry. Be happy that he is not sick and suffering and that he is with Lord Narayana. I will miss him, and I am sorry that you did not get to see him." Brave as those words were, I could sense the emotion behind them. "When we did not hear from you we knew that we had not reached you in time," she continued. " So, on Tuesday, yesterday, we cremated his body." Matter-of-fact words from a strong woman who had just lost the man who was her whole world.

"Amma, I don't have a visa permit to come home. If I can get it in a couple of days, I'll try to be there. I'll come as soon as I can."

"No, môl. I will be all right. I have Shanthi and Sarada-akkan here for me. Your Daddy is not here anymore. He wanted to see you and the girls, but it is too late."

"I am sorry, Amma." I did not know what else to say.

Amma said firmly. "Don't come now. Come when your papers are all o.k. Just pray for his soul, and pray for me. Give the girls and Balu my love."

She hung up. Strong in her belief in God, she had already guided me to take care of my family who needed me.

*"Pray for his soul,"* she says matter-of-factly. Of course... but, how do I pray? My whole being is shaken up. I can't think. How can I pray?

My mother had my brother and sisters beside her to grieve with.

Even if I left on a special visa, I would have arrived there at least six or seven days after my father was gone. It would only start another round of wailing and tears and my visit with my mother would not mean anything, overshadowed by the tragedy of my father's death.

I did not go.

# 41

## *A Remembrance to My Daddy*

### *Because*

Because I left without
saying goodbye
never again did you see me

because the call of the west
took me away

because the oceans came
between us
never did I hear you
ever again

because the moon and the sun
rose and set without fail
and the earth kept on turning
never did time stop
to let me return

never could I look after your needs
because I did not return
and tend your ailing heart

your loving words
I heard no more

And never did I say
a real goodbye.

Goodbyes can be different.

Some are "see you later" goodbyes, and some are "never again" goodbyes. You never know which it is when you say "goodbye."

The night before I left India in January, 1964 to come to the States, I had dinner with my daddy and his best friend from grade school, *Rajan Maaman,* Rajan Uncle, in Bombay, India.

Later the same night I said goodbye to my dad at the Bombay Airport.

*January 30, 1964*

*That was the last time I saw my dear Dad and his famous white beard.*

On September 27th, 1970, I was having dinner with the same Rajan Maaman, this time at his daughter's house in Evanston, Illinois. We talked about *their* good old days, and we talked about how when we were young Daddy took us to visit Rajan Maaman and family at the Army Headquarters in our hometown. Even as we shared fond memories of him, my daddy had died at home, in Trivandrum. It was already the morning of September 28th there. I had not seen my daddy for six years and eight months since I said goodbye to him at the Bombay Airport.

What happened to me in the interim changed my life forever. In more ways than I could have imagined. I completed my training in pathology, started my medical practice in the field of Pathology and Laboratory Medicine, and was raising two beautiful daughters. My husband, Raj, was in a group practice with two other internal medicine doctors. We were awaiting our permanent visas to settle down in the States. While our visas were pending, we had not been able to go back to see our families. My girls had never met their *Appooppa*.

I realized too late that goodbyes can be of different kinds. When I said 'goodbye' to my dad in 1964, it was said with full intention of returning to India after five years of residency training in our respective fields, and settling down in our hometown amidst family and friends. I never did say a final goodbye to my dad.

Yes, Daddy, I did leave you and my special days with you, unaware that I would never see you again.

I came away from a place of deep confidence, partly from the nurturing of Ammoomma, Amma, Ammachi and Adukkala Ammoomma, but eighty percent of it came from you. You deeply instilled the notion in me that I was a goddess and how the spirit of the divine flowed within me. I could do anything, and I could do no wrong.

The townspeople knew you as K.V. Sivaraam, the best photographer in town. In my mind you were the best photographer in the world. The scenes in your pictures always showed *caring* in the family portraits, and when you took the group pictures of a graduating class you made sure each face showed the *pride* in his or her graduation by capturing the essence of a worthwhile educational experience. There was a belief in town that when a girl's photo was taken in your studio for the purpose of an arranged marriage, a good alliance and a great marriage occurred within the same year. I came to recognize the divine power in you which made that happen. Your heart and soul went into your work, always, and I am sure that the forces of the universe felt them.

You taught me how to be gracious. From the ruling Maharajah in Trivandrum when I was young, to Pandit Jawaharlal Nehru when he visited our town after India's independence from the British, you were the one called upon to take the official portraits. No one else would do. When the liberated India became the Indian Union, and changed our Maharajah to a Rajpramukh, and converted him to just a figure-head with no ruling powers, you showed him the respect as in previous days when he was the sole head of state. When our state of Travancore was merged with the northern parts to form the new Kerala State, with a welcome smile and a kind word, you took the pictures of the officials that descended upon us from the north. Even as a teenager I took pride in your accommodating attitude and tolerance of the strangers who came to town.

I learned compassion through you. You did not have a bank account. Many in our family disapproved of the fact that, while you made a lot of money in your photo studio, you kept little of what you earned. They said you squandered the money on relatives and friends. I know very well that you always had at least two people under your wing at any time whom you put through college or trade school. Some were immediate family, some distant, and some were children of friends from out of town. Taking care of them cost plenty of money, and you were generous to a fault. Many a time you gave your last rupee to a nephew or a friend's daughter because he or she needed to make a trip home.

You gave me the gift of laughter. Many a time, as I rush to get to work or some other place, I hear your remark from ages ago: *"Yennte mukkothipennu,"* my fishmonger-girl. You were referring to the unique fashion in which the fisherwomen walked. Wide woven baskets filled to the brim with the fresh catch of the day were placed on their heads, and it was a fine balancing act as they walked very fast to sell their wares from door to door. To balance the fish-baskets on their heads, they swung both arms back and forth, and as they did so, their behinds swung out in a not-so-modest waddle. You called me a *mukkothi-pen-nu*, because I walked with both my arms swinging back and forth like the *fish-monger women* walked. You thought it very funny that I shook my behind like they did and teased me for it, although at five or ten I had not acquired much of a behind to speak of, and you need not have worried about immodesty.

You often said that I talked too fast. When I told a story, you tried to slow me down by raising your palm to interrupt me with, "Stop the train. Allow me to get aboard." You made me laugh. I would stop, take a deep breath, and tell my story over again, with all the commas and full stops. Afterwards, you hugged me and laughed with me.

When I left Trivandrum to join Raj in Chicago, I was twenty-three years old, and you were a strapping young 54-year-old with a beard that demanded respect, and a stride that walked everywhere unafraid. How would I know your diabetes would catch up with you before I could return home to you? I wish I had the chance. I still miss your voice and I still miss the way you came into a room humming the songs of Lord Krishna. A warm smile on your face and a prayer on your lips, is how I remember you. My daddy, my father, my mentor and my friend. I still miss you.

# Epilogue

**LIFE LESSONS ARE** only learned by living them. Facing the challenges in my life, I delved deep into myself and remembered how my Ammoomma, Dad, Mom, and Ammachi loved, lived, and nurtured family through good times and tough times. Maybe because I was plucked away from the warm, cozy place and literally thrown out into a cold world, I worked hard to make my place a warm one, and always strove to cherish people in my life.

The lessons I learned in my early years have withstood the passage of time and helped me stay strong all my life.

In 1974, Molly came into our lives, and Raj and I gained one more beautiful, vibrant daughter.

As my girls grew, two sons-in-law, Devi's husband Don, Molly's husband Suresh, enlarged our family. Devi's two sons, Niko and Travis added abundant joy and literally became the focus in all our lives.

Over the years, with the addition of many siblings and families we have grown to over fifty members.

I have encouraged the next generations to gain knowledge and strength from our faith and culture to enrich their lives.

Raj and I have been blessed to be able to go back and visit our people and places where we came from, with our family on many occasions

I am happy to share some of those moments in this memoir.
Namasté

January 1998.    Return visit to Hill View, the home we left to come to
the States. Don, Devi, Niko, Shaku, Raj and Nimmi.

1998  Trivandrum, India.
Don, Devi, Nimmi, Raj,  Shaku, Niko, Molly, Suresh

January 1998.  Our family in Agra when we visited the TajMahal.
Don, Devi, Niko, Shanthi, Nimmi, Pooja, Shaku, Molly, Suresh, Raj.

1998,    My Grandson Niko visiting a 28 year old elephant, Anil.

2013,　My grandson Travis visiting a 10-year-old elephant,
*Peroor Krishnan.*

2013  Don, Devi, Travis

2013  Travis in Agra

2009  Niko, Devi, Don, Shaku, Raj, Nimmi, Molly, Suresh

# Acknowledgements

I WISH TO express my gratitude to my family and friends who individually and collectively helped shape me in my life and form my memories. Without all of you I would not have these stories to tell.

Devi and Don, Molly and Suresh, Nimmi, Niko and Maria, have listened patiently to my readings and my rantings. Travis heard with deep interest all about my ammoomma and my dad, Sivaraam Appoo, over the many sleepovers with me. My loving *'thank yous'* to all of you.

Over many years, my friends at Barrington Writers Workshop helped contour my book with their constructive critiques. Helen Gallagher, April Williams and Michelle Mathis have kept me on track and my pages in order so I can share them with the world. Thank you. Raj, our love gave me the courage to document your stories and how they became mine. I close my eyes and see you smiling at me. I pray for your blessings to our young ones.

Namasté

*Glossary*

| | |
|---|---|
| Lord Ganesha | Hindu deity who gets rid of obstacles to any endeavors, and assures success. |
| Lord Brahma | The creator.<br><br>Regardless of the main attributable qualities, Hindus believe that all Gods are one and called by any name the god-power manifests to help our mortal lives. Also the divinity within us is a manifestation of the Universal God Power. |
| Lord Vishnu | The Sustainer. In his avatar on earth, known as Lord Krishna |
| Lord Shiva | The destroyer, and a second one in the Triumvirate. Without destruction, new things cannot emerge. A very powerful God, who issues boons to people who pray ardently to Shiva. |
| Devi | Goddess |
| Lekshmi Devi | Goddess Lekshmi is Lord Vishnu's consort and brings health, wealth and happiness to devotees. |

| Parvathi Devi | Goddess Parvathi is Lord Shiva's wife and in that form is the Goddess of Love and Devotion. |
| | To destroy cruel demons and to save the world from evil, Parvathi takes the warrior forms of Durga or Kali |
| Saraswathi Devi | Goddess of all education including music, she is revered by students and pursuers of knowledge. |
| Pooja | Pooja or Puja is a prayer ritual by Hindus in which water, flowers, fruits and food items are offered to a deity of choice. Usually cotton wicks in an oil-lamp are lit to represent offering of *Agni*, or fire. |
| Aarti | As part of a pooja ritual a metal tray, (usually a brass tray,) with an oil lamp or lit pieces of camphor is waved around the idol of the deity and then offered to devotees to get the blessing of the ceremonial lamp to each individual. |
| Ashram | A place of seclusion where Hindu members share spiritual goals and practices, and time devoted to prayer and meditation. |
| Ammoomma | Grandmother |
| Amma | Mother, Mom |
| Achan | Father, Dad |
| Ammachi | That is what I called my *Valiamma*, my mother's older sister |
| Valiachan | Father's older brother or Valiamma's husband. |

| Trivandrum | Our hometown city where Raj and I grew up. The name has been reverted to the original native version *'Thiruvananthapuram.'* |
| --- | --- |
| Sambar | A mixed vegetable curry with potatoes, yellow split peas, onions, cucumbers etc. and seasoned with coriander, red pepper, salt, asafoetida, foenugreek and tamarind water. To top it off, black mustard seeds, red chili peppers and curry leaves are fired in hot oil and layered on top.<br><br>Sambar served atop rice or dosa. |
| Avial | A mixed vegetable dish of raw bananas, cucumbers, eggplant, green peppers, drumsticks etc. Grated coconut, cumin, turmeric salt are added, and topped off with curry leaves, a couple of spoons of yougurt and a tablespoon of oil. |
| Dosa | Breakfast food. A thin pancake of batter made from soaked rice and black gram. The batter is left to rise overnight before the pancakes are made on the griddle. They are also served with a savored potato filling called potato masala. |
| Idli | Steamed rice cakes made of batter very similar to the above mentioned dosa batter, but thicker in order to steam the rice cakes |
| Dharma | Customary duty of a Hindu. A duty to behave according to strict religious and social codes, including righteousness. |
| Gandhiji | A respectful term used to address Mahatma Gandhi. |

CPSIA information can be obtained
at www.ICGtesting.com
Printed in the USA
BVHW091931211019
561686BV00001B/2/P